Happy Birthday

MONET

Lots of love
Marta ✚ ✚ ✚

MONET

Jean-Paul Crespelle

HAZAN

Cover illustration
Monet, On the Beach at Trouville, 1870.
Musée Marmottan, Paris.

Translation
Jane Brenton

Design
Anne Anquetil

© Fernand Hazan, Paris 1986
© SPADEM
Printed in Italy

ISBN 2-85025-108-6

'Monet's a halfwit!' declared Georges Braque to Jean Bazaine, in 1950. This opinion had been voiced by the avant-garde artists at the turn of the century, and earlier by Odilon Redon, who accused the Impressionists of being 'weak in the head'. Redon mentioned no artist by name, but Claude Monet, the ultimate Impressionist, may have been the subject of his ridicule. Redon continued: 'Anything that could transcend or illuminate or amplify the object, anything that pertained to the sphere of mystery, doubt or delicious unease, was to them a closed book.' As Cézanne put it: 'Monet is just an eye.'

However, there were others who took the opposite view. Kandinsky, who was dazzled by the *Haystacks* he saw in Munich, that wrote: 'The painting seemed to me vested with a miraculous power. But insensibly the "object" used in the work, although it was an indispensable element, began to dwindle in importance in my eyes.' Later, the Abstract Expressionists were to find in Monet's work a similar justification for the approach they adopted to painting.

These very different reactions illustrate how, from his debut at the Salon in 1865 up to his death in 1926, Monet attracted both adulation and controversy. The harsh judgements offered by Castagnary, Albert Wolf and Huysmans were securely based, and it was many years before the venomous personal attacks ceased and were obscured by the enthusiasm of Zola, Astruc, Duranty and Edmond Maître.

However, the fury of the attacks launched on him by others was minor compared to the severity with which Monet judged his own work. He was mercilessly self-critical, lamenting always his lack of ability and denigrating and even destroying what he produced. In the course of his life he slashed or burned literally hundreds of landscapes because he thought them failures. Just six months before he died he burned sixty paintings. René Gimpel tells us that he visited him in November 1918 and found him in total despair. 'Painting causes me too much suffering, 'Monet told him, 'there's everything in the past I'm not satisfied with, and the sheer impossibility of getting it right every time. Yes, every time I start a canvas I think I'm going to create a masterpiece, and it never, ever happens. It's appalling, never being satisfied. I suffer terribly.' He was seventy-eight and his reputation was at its peak.

His own self-doubt was only exacerbated by the praise heaped on him by others, whether casual admirers or famous men of letters such as Zola, Maupassant, Octave Mirbeau, Mallarmé or Geffroy, who hailed him as one of the masters of French painting. To Geffroy, his self-appointed publicist, he declared: '... all the compliments I have received are out of proportion and I think of the works of the great masters who have revealed to us such harmonious and magnificent creations: Titian, Veronese, Rubens, Velasquez, Rembrandt, men whose genius is beyond all doubt. What are our paintings, what are my paintings compared to theirs?'

Monet was glad to receive recognition, but even in his most euphoric moments—and there were many —he was never confident of his own talent. Sensitive, lacking assurance, easily hurt, the least setback or failure would plunge him into the depths of despair—his reaction so intense that it would have been ridiculous were it not so genuinely heartfelt. His extensive correspondence is little more than a litany of complaints: artistic problems, money worries, changes in the weather, hotel food... When things were really on top of him he would simply go home and sleep. The family would go about on tiptoe, afraid to rouse him.

In fact his problems, whether artistic or practical, were no greater than those experienced by the majority of the independent artists of his day. Renoir, Pissarro and Sisley endured equally difficult periods in their lives and did not

The Young Monet.

complain half as much. Monet took everything to heart, and yet this short, stocky, solidly-built man—only 1 metre 65 tall—had the constitution of an ox, and thought nothing of painting out-of-doors in winter snow or buffeted by the storms of Belle-Ile or in temperatures of minus 25° in Norway.

Tenacious and determined in everything connected with his work, he could also be a complete coward. In 1867 he retreated to the comfort of his family home in Le Havre, leaving his mistress Camille to face childbirth alone and penniless. Three years later, frightened of conscription, he fled to London. The unfortunate Camille, now with a young child, was left to make her own arrangements to join him in England.

In the last analysis one can judge Monet only in terms of his vocation as a painter. Everything else in his life was secondary to his work. His passion for painting was stronger than love or friendship, so that he often seemed insensitive to the needs of others. It made him neglect those he loved and who gave him constant support and encouragement, while receiving little or no thanks in return. He was a man obsessed. 'Nothing in the world interests me except my painting and my flowers,' he once said.

When you try to build up a picture of Monet's character from his letters and the accounts left by his family and few close friends, you discover an introverted and rather silent man, content to let others do the talking but absorbing and using everything he heard.

From his stepdaughter Blanche in particular, we know he could be violent, flying into a rage if crossed, capable of kicking a picture that displeased him until it was damaged beyond repair. Some have concluded that he was a rough, uneducated man, a sort of naive genius, but that is far from correct. His massive correspondence proves that he wrote well, read the great writers of the day and possessed excellent critical judgement. The truth is that he was a solitary, the prisoner of his own passion; although he was a major figure on the artistic scene and played a crucial role in the emergence of Impressionism, he had few real friends. You could count them on the fingers of two hands: Courbet, first, to whom he remained loyal even after his imprisonment and disgrace; Manet, for whom his admiration and affection were undimmed; Renoir, a friend since his student days, and the only one of the Impressionists to whom he used the familiar form 'tu'; Rodin, his exact contemporary; Cézanne, another friend since his youth, with whom he sometimes argued spectacularly; Pissarro, one of the few artists he helped financially when his own luck turned: and finally, perhaps surprisingly, Whistler —proof that opposites attract each other.

In respect of Monet's love-life, there is frankly little of interest to relate. Apart from his two wives, the lovely Camille who died at the age of thirty-two, and Alice Hoschedé, who shared with him both hardship and success, apart from them we know only of a brief youthful flirtation with a girl called Eugénie. Like Renoir, to quote Jeanne Samary, Claude Monet 'made love only with his paintbrush'. In all his work there is not the least hint of sensuality, he never in his life painted a nude.

Monet was not unaffectionate: he loved his family and took pains over his children's education, worried about their health and future happiness. Although he had a well-deserved reputation for meanness, he made sure they were well provided for and comfortable. A marked contrast to his attitude to friends who helped him out of trouble—they rarely received so much as a painting in return.

For himself he asked little, although he liked well-cut clothes of good quality, English tweed suits and fine lawn shirts with embroidered cuffs. His only vice, if it can be said to be one, was a love of good food. Even in times of acute financial embarrassment he never neglected his stomach. When he wrote to Duret trying to borrow a hundred francs, he also asked him to send a keg of brandy.

But it was painting that was always at the centre of his thoughts: what subjects to choose, how to approach them and, almost equally important, how to sell his work to dealers and collectors. It is astonishing how many business letters were written by a man who worked out-of-doors or in his studio from dawn till dusk—and in the summer that meant rising at 3.30 a. m. Every night before he went to bed he wrote, by lamplight, to his dealers and friends, asking for money, setting up exhibitions or an auction sale, or simply deferring payment to the man who sold him his materials.

In all this vast correspondence there are numerous references to Monet's dissatisfaction with his work, but scarcely any discussion of aesthetics or techniques. 'I paint as the bird sings,' Monet said—misleadingly. Certainly he painted fast, working often on ten canvases at a time, but he usually took great pains in choosing his subjects which, once fixed, he would paint as they were, without modification. His letters echo with despairing cries at not finding the right motif or the exact vantage point he wanted. And if the leaves turned brown or the grass was too green or had been cut, for him that was a catastrophe.

About his painting techniques he was no more forthcoming. In that respect it is convenient to divide his work into two main periods: before Vétheuil (where he lived from 1878-81) and after Vétheuil. Before Vétheuil he used a light-coloured palette to paint landscapes in which water, sky, mist, snow and clouds predominate. After making a preliminary drawing in charcoal, his method was to apply little dabs of colour, instinctively observing the colour theories of Chevreul on the division of tones. Or alternatively, he would use broad expanses of flat colour laid on in thin washes, treating oil paints as though they

were watercolours. Sometimes he employed both techniques within the one canvas.

The post-Vétheuil period was marked by a quite different treatment of landscape, from which human figures have almost entirely disappeared. This was the era of the series, which gave Monet the opportunity to study, with quite extraordinary visual acuity, the variations in colour exhibited by a single object, depending on how it was affected by light, the season, the weather or the time of day. Undoubtedly it is in these series that Claude Monet makes his most personal statement and his most significant contribution to modern art. With the series of *Haystacks, Poplars* and *Rouen Cathedral*, leading up to the *Waterlilies*, he attained a freedom of style that opened the way for the Fauves and, ultimately, the Abstract Expressionists. He was also recognized as the undisputed leader of the Impressionist group, 'le grand patron', as Octave Mirbeau described him.

Every history of Impressionism stresses the difficulties encountered by the individuals in the group at the outset of their careers. And with reason. No previous artistic movement had aroused such hostility that its members had to wait twenty years or more for their contribution to be recognized and their talent acknowledged.

The situation in which painting found itself in France during the mid-nineteenth century is somewhat complex. Art had become institutionalized, it was an 'official' activity and artists occupied more or less the position of civil servants. Purchases, commissions, appointments, awards, all were in the gift of the state; it was impossible to make a career outside the system unless you had a private income (as was the case with Manet, Degas, Morisot and, up to a point, Cézanne, who received an allowance from his father). If you were poor then you had to be prepared to struggle—and that was possibly more painful for Monet than for most as he had grown up in bourgeois comfort and was not equipped to deal with hardship.

The system functioned like a well-oiled and efficient machine, picking up the young artist at the start of his career and processing him through the various stages: École des Beaux-Arts, Prix de Rome, a period at the Villa Médicis, a medal at the Salon. A first prize brought with it automatically the award of the Légion d'Honneur and a teaching post. For the practising artist the vital hurdle to be overcome was acceptance at the Salon. In an era when the picture dealers of Paris could be counted on one hand, the Salon was the only place where an artist could exhibit and become known to the critics and the general public. It was also the only means he had of selling his works and making a living. Usually the award of a medal meant that the state would purchase the picture, and there would be commissions from private individuals. It was a crazy and unfair system, and was bitterly attacked by artists outside it, such as Ingres, Delacroix and Courbet.

Even under Napoleon III the academic artists received vast numbers of state commissions. But in the early years of the Third Republic, in the aftermath of the destruction wrought by the Franco-Prussian War and the Commune, building-sites were springing up everywhere. In Paris alone there was the Opéra to finish, and the new walls of the Hôtel de Ville had to be decorated, also the Sorbonne, the Cour des Comptes, etc. It was the same on a smaller scale in the provincial towns. The process of reconstruction continued right up to the outbreak of the First World War —forty years of lucrative commissions for the 'professional' artists.

One can therefore understand all too well why the academic painters who stood to gain from this largesse (the 'pompiers' or 'hacks' as they were known) looked so askance at the arrival on the scene of a new group of young painters, who were outside the official network but who had the potential to compete for the same favours. They obstructed the newcomers at every turn, cloaking their rejections in a barrage of technical and aesthetic criticism that was no more than a disguise for their own venality and greed. *Plein-air* painting, light colours, the representation of modern life, these were nothing more nor less than an abomination!

To halt the advance of the young painters, with their pretended humility, they strengthened their hold over the Salon jury and the press, who were complete innocents in artistic matters and content to trust the judgement of the experts. There were three of them in particular who spearheaded the campaign: Cabanel, painter of a *Birth of Venus* exhibited at the Salon of 1865 opposite Manet's *Olympia*—it was bought by the Emperor for 50,000 francs; Gérôme, married to the daughter of the art dealer Goupil, owner of the most prestigious gallery in Paris; and Bonnat, who taught Toulouse-Lautrec and himself painted forbidding portraits of politicians for which he was paid fabulous sums. Cabanel faded from the scene, but Gérôme and Bonnat maintained the attack until the early years of the next century. At the International Exhibition of 1900, when Impressionism had long since won the day, they rushed up to President Loubet as he was about to visit an exhibition of their work and shouted: 'Stop, Monsieur le Président! This is France's shame.'

The most curious aspect of the whole affair is that, initially, the Impressionists were not opposed to the École des Beaux-Arts or the Salon. Most of them were taught at some point by one of the Beaux-Arts teachers, and indeed the first thing Monet did when he arrived in Paris was seek out Troyon, a medal winner, and ask for his advice. Troyon recommended him to enrol with Thomas Couture, Manet's teacher, but in the event Monet chose to attend the prestigious studio run by Gleyre. There he met

Renoir, who was to become a lifelong friend.   All any of them ever hoped for was to exhibit at the Salon.   According to Jacques-Émile Blanche, every brushstroke Manet ever painted was dedicated to that end.   Cézanne dreamed all his life of having a canvas accepted for the Salon, and he was finally admitted in 1882, as an act of kindness. Monet's aims were no different.   His early seascapes won him a place in the Salon of 1865, as did the following year his portrait of Camille, which was greeted with such enthusiasm that he hoped to make a successful career as a portraitist and become another Carolus Duran.   He met with rejections in 1867 and 1869, however, and in disgust submitted nothing more for ten years.   When he tried again in 1880, this time successfully, he found that his fine landscape of Lavacourt had been hung at a height of six metres and was virtually invisible.

The hostility of the establishment was further fuelled by the flattering articles written about the independents by Émile Zola, who enjoyed the reputation of being a young hothead.   His championing of the Impressionist cause was linked to a general attack on bourgeois values.   When he saw the portrait of Camille at the Salon and wrote in *L'Événement* that, compared with Monet, all the other painters were eunuchs ('Ah yes, there is spirit, there is a man in a crowd of eunuchs!'), then the fat was truly in the fire.   Pressure was put on the editor of the magazine and the headstrong journalist was asked to leave.   He continued however to support the Impressionists, until the day when his own fame and fortune was assured and, youthful ardour spent, he began to revise his views.   His final verdict on the Impressionists was that they were geniuses who had failed to fulfil their promise.   He wrote a novel called *L'Œuvre*, the sad hero of which, Claude Lantier, is a sort of amalgam of Manet and Monet, with a little of Cézanne thrown in.   Nevertheless, at the time of his death the pictures given him by Monet still hung on his walls,
while the twelve Cézannes had been relegated to the attic.

During the twenty years in which Impressionism was forced to prove itself, there were of course lulls in the hostilities, and often alliances formed between the two sides. Manet, for example, painted a portrait of Carolus Duran, whose success he respected; Degas had known Octave Mirbeau and Bonnat since his youth, and he continued to see them regularly; Monet was a close friend of Helleu—indeed Marcel Proust probably had this friendship in mind when he created the painter Elstir in *Remembrance of Things Past.*   Proust knew Monet's work through his friend Madame Straus and there are long accounts of his paintings and his garden—which he had never seen—in *Jean Santeuil*.

Because of the distance at which he lived from Paris, Monet had less occasion than most to mingle with the artistic establishment.   Nevertheless they regarded him as their prime target, promulgator of the Impressionist heresy with all its attendant dangers.   In a sense, of course, they were perfectly correct.   The movement was a threat—for them.   In 1890 Claude Monet was famous, no one seriously doubted his talent, while the 'professionals' who had kept him in poverty for so long were beginning their descent down the slippery slope to oblivion.

Oscar-Claude Monet was born in Paris on 14 November 1840, but the birth of the painter Monet occurred on the Normandy coast in 1858, an event presided over by Eugène Boudin, eighteen years Monet's senior, the painter whom Corot dubbed the 'king of skies'.   In a picture-framer's shop in Le Havre, where some of his own paintings were on display, Boudin had noticed a number of caricatures of local celebrities done by the young Monet. 'You should try painting,' he told him when they met.   It took some time to persuade the young man, who saw his drawings simply as a useful way of supplementing his allowance.   'I nearly died of pride,' he said later.   And

Renoir : La Grenouillère, 1869.

so, one summer's day, he set off with Boudin to paint out-doors, an idea he initially found unattractive. But he quickly mastered the principles of landscape painting and the use of a gamut of light colours, and developed a fascination with the sea and water that was to last all his life. He once asked that his dead body should be laid to rest in a buoy, surrounded by the element he loved.

Monet's initiation was completed two years later when he met Jongkind on the cliffs at Sainte-Adresse. The Dutch painter was a bohemian figure who used to wander about the estuary, painting often in Le Havre or Honfleur. Like Boudin before him, he took Monet with him on his painting expeditions.

At the time he met Jongkind, Monet was convalescing from an attack of typhoid picked up in Algeria, where he had served ten months in the light cavalry. Although he had enjoyed his time in Africa, he never returned to complete his tour of duty because his wealthy aunt Lecadre decided to pay for a substitute, a practice then current. It probably explains why Monet felt that the war in 1870 had very little to do with him.

Jongkind was a subtle stylist and his teaching complemented that of Boudin. Monet was never to forget the debt he owed him, and he told a journalist who interviewed him in 1900: 'He asked me to go along and work with him, explained the whys and wherefores of his style, and in this way completed the education I had received from Boudin. From that moment he became my true master, and it was to him that I owed the definitive training of my eye.'

These formative years on the Normandy coast and by the banks of the Seine were full of new experiences. Because of them he was able, with his family's help, to enrol as a pupil of Charles Gleyre, recommended by a genre painter called Toulmouche who was related to his aunt. Gleyre was a straightforward and good-natured man (Renoir described him as an idiot with a Teutonic accent—he was in

fact Swiss) and he tried patiently but with little success to guide Monet towards an academic style of drawing. 'You're not thinking of the classical models,' he used to say. But it was hardly the approach likely to appeal to a young painter whose eye had been liberated by the example and advice of Boudin and Jongkind. At Easter 1863, Monet gathered together his friends in the studio, Renoir, Bazille and Sisley, and said: 'Let's get out of this place, it's not healthy, there's a lack of sincerity here!' And off they all went to Chailly, near the Forest of Fontainebleau, where they stayed in an inn recommended by Gleyre, who apparently bore them no ill will.

Monet loved the place and returned there often, either alone or with friends, to paint in the forest or on the Chailly road. But his major preoccupation in those years was the planning and execution of two vast canvases. One was *Le Déjeuner sur l'herbe* (1865), a tribute to Manet whose revolutionary canvas of that name he had seen and admired at the Salon des Refusés of 1863; the other, painted two years later, was the no less ambitious *Women in the Garden*, in which he attempted to capture the effect of light falling in patches on figures in the shade of trees. *Le Déjeuner sur l'herbe* was in the end left unfinished. The vast composition, six metres long, posed too many problems, and Monet must have been discouraged by the friendly criticisms offered by Courbet, who had determined to meet this young man who, he heard, 'painted something other than angels'. *Women in the Garden* was started in the grounds of the house Monet had rented in Sèvres, on the proceeds of the sale of his portrait of Camille (which he painted in the interval between his two larger canvases and sold to Arsène Houssaye, former director of the Comédie-Française, for the quite unexpected sum of 800 francs). The large garden picture was bought by Bazille for 2,500 francs, payable in monthly instalments of 50 francs—an arrangement which caused continual wrangling over late payment.

Monet : La Grenouillère, 1869.

Unsatisfied with these pieces of 'engineering', compositions dominated by figures dressed like fashionplates, Monet turned resolutely to landscapes. It was a struggle to keep going. He owed the village butcher 300 francs and had to leave Sèvres almost overnight, destroying 200 canvases before he went rather than let them be seized by the bailiffs. In spite of his precautions the canvases were patched up and sold off as job lots at thirty francs per bundle of fifty.

Monet's young companion Camille, seven years his junior, was forced to give birth to her first son Jean in appalling circumstances. She was alone and without money and her only support came from a friend who was a medical student. Claude had gone to Le Havre to make his peace with his father and, above all, his aunt, who was shocked at his goings-on and threatened to cut off his allowance. It was during this visit, in the summer of 1867, that he painted the famous *Terrace at Sainte-Adresse*, which shows his father and aunt in the garden looking out to sea.

Monet's financial pressures abated somewhat for a few weeks in the following spring, when one of his paintings was accepted for the Salon. He went with Camille and the baby to stay at the inn in a tiny village called Gloton, on the banks of the Seine opposite Bonnières. It was a remote spot, approached by crossing the river in an ancient ferryboat attached to a chain, but what awaited you was a paradise of fresh green meadows, buttercups and dragonflies.

In the squalid inn, eating the dreadful food—as Zola and Cézanne had done two years before—Monet spent many happy hours with Camille, a halcyon interlude that is wonderfully evoked in *The River*, today in the Art Institute of Chicago, probably the first painting that is totally Impressionist in spirit. All the elements are there: water, iridescence, reflections, pale colours, coloured shadows and, above all, that atmosphere of euphoria that is the movement's hallmark.

After the peace and quiet of Gloton it was time to face reality again. Apparently that reality was so grim that Monet threw himself into the river—so at least he wrote in the postscript of a letter to Bazille. However Jean-Pierre Hoschedé categorically denies this can be true, and points out that Monet was brought up by the sea and was an excellent swimmer; if he had indeed tried to drown himself he would have instinctively swum to safety.

In 1869, Monet and his family went to live in the village of Saint-Michel, near Bougival. They had reached rock bottom. There was no money coming from Monet's family, and Monsieur Gaudibert's generous gift had barely covered the expense of moving. Monet appealed to Bazille for help, but in the meantime he and his family were literally starving. Renoir was living with his parents at nearby Louveciennes, and he used to raid the larder, fill his pockets with bread and take it to his friends. He too wrote to Bazille, emphasizing Monet's plight: 'I am at my parents', and most of the time at Monet's house, where incidentally things are getting serious. They don't eat every day.'

The appeals to Bazille, then in Montpellier with his family, were obviously sincere. Yet Monet, while berating his friend for being slow in paying his monthly instalment of fifty francs, also asked him to send a barrel of wine from the family estate. 'At least we won't drink so much water, and it will be a great saving.' That sums up a great deal about the man.

Another paradox. Painting in Bougival, often in Renoir's company, Monet produced some of the most tranquil and happy pictures of his career, notably those of the 'Grenouillère'. This floating café was on a backwater of the River Seine, looking across to the Ile de Croissy. Its clientèle consisted largely of young people who came there to swim or row. In an era when transport was restricted, Chatou, Bougival and Croissy were within easy reach by train from Paris. On fine days a laughing crowd would descend on the pleasant spot by the river, presenting an animated and brilliant spectacle. Monet delighted in painting the scene, which Maupassant too described with delight when he discovered the place in 1873. But above all he liked to paint the river itself, expressing his intoxication with the water and wonderfully recreating its changing pattern of reflections, its transparent sheen. Émile Zola wrote in *L'Événement Illustré*: 'Monet is one of the few painters who can paint water without inane effects of transparency or fake reflections. In his work the water is alive, deep and, above all, real. It slaps against the boats in little greenish spurts shot with white gleams. It is not at all the artificial crystal-pure water of the armchair seascape painters.'

In that year of 1869, whenever Monet had a few francs in his pocket—usually from his rich Le Havre patron Monsieur Gaudibert, whose wife's portrait he had painted—he would seize the opportunity to go to Paris, and in particular to pay a visit to a certain café.

The group of young independents had fallen into the habit of meeting up in the evenings at the Café Guerbois, a modest establishment frequented by Manet, in the Grand'Rue des Batignolles, today the Avenue de Clichy. Every Friday they would all try to be there, Renoir, Sisley, Pissarro, Degas, Cézanne, Bazille and Monet. There might be the opportunity to discuss painting with, say, Zola, or the engraver Desboutins, the musician Cabaner, or Duranty, the essayist and champion of realism who preached the need to represent modern life in art. Among the expanding group there would often be a few friendly establishment figures, such as Alfred Stevens, Gervex, Guillemet or Cazin. On his frequent visits to Paris, Whistler would enliven the proceedings with his acid witticisms.

Monet admired Whistler's spirit, but he himself contributed little, preferring to sit in silence, sipping his beer and puffing at his pipe. He had always been a reticent man and he genuinely liked listening to what the others had to say, learning much from the elegant and trenchant arguments advanced by Manet and Degas, men of the world whose education was far superior to his own, or from the more acrimonious exchanges between Monet and Cézanne, who profoundly disliked one another.

In those years preceding the Franco-Prussian War, the Guerbois was the melting-pot in which the theories of Impressionism were refined, amidst clouds of pipesmoke and to the accompaniment of clicking billiard balls. Monet's contribution to the debate was minimal; he preferred to find his expression on canvas. And, working alone, intuitive rather than theoretical, he arrived at a style of painting that summed up the essential spirit of Impressionism.

Monet was in Trouville on 19 July 1870, the fateful day when Napoleon III fell into Bismarck's trap and declared war on Prussia. Monet was unconcerned. His aunt had paid for a substitute who would be enlisted in his place, and he felt no stirrings of patriotic fervour. In that respect his reaction was not unlike Cézanne's. He too had a substitute, paid for by his wealthy father, and his first act on hearing news of the hostilities was to leave for Estaque with his latest conquest, a former model of his called Henriette Fiquet. The purpose of the trip was to join Zola who, as the only son of a widow, was not subject to conscription, and who was spending his honeymoon in the little fishing village near Marseille. Events moved so rapidly towards defeat that the fighting was over by the time the authorities in Aix received orders to apprehend Cézanne.

In the early months of that summer Monet had produced several canvases notable for their light-hearted holiday spirit. Perhaps recalling Boudin's success with beach scenes, he painted a number of views of the promenade, the Hôtel des Roches-Noires (later Proust's model for the Hôtel de Balbec), charming scenes of Camille in light summer clothes sitting with Jean on the beach. They were visions of a carefree age that was about to be swept away.

Monet began to worry only when Gambetta set about raising a new army of 500,000 men. Strong, and bursting with rude health, he felt increasingly anxious that he would be conscripted. Already, when he was painting on the beach, he attracted disapproving glances from people who thought he was on the run. A lot of painters and writers shared his unease, and the late summer of 1870 saw a general exodus from the country. In the face of the advancing army, Pissarro had been forced to flee from his house in Louveciennes to take refuge in Brittany, before going on to London to stay with his half-sister. Daubigny, Bonvin and Sisley were already in England—although the latter, being English, was merely acting prudently in returning to his native soil. Boudin and Diaz were in two minds whether to leave, but eventually made their way to Brussels, where they knew a number of collectors who would give them shelter.

Only Manet and Degas enrolled in the National Guard, their patriotism aroused by the humiliating defeats suffered by France. Renoir was sent to join the cavalry but was discharged at Tarbes.

An atmosphere of general panic had overtaken Le Havre, when Monet went there to find out the latest news. The shipping company offices were literally besieged with people desperate to leave for England. Caught up in the confusion, Monet must have lost his head. On an impulse he boarded ship and left. Never for one instant did he think of himself as a deserter. Worse still, he did not spare a thought for Camille and the baby, left without money in Trouville, the hotel bill unpaid. It was only by some miracle that his young wife of a few weeks found a way to join him soon afterwards.

Against all expectations, affairs in London took a turn for the better. Only a few days after he arrived, Monet met Daubigny in a café used by the French exiles. He was in excellent spirits, living comfortably and painting views of the Thames that were much sought after by English collectors. When he learned of the predicament of the talented young painter, whom he had always supported—even resigning from the Salon jury when they rejected one of his paintings—he lost no time in effecting an introduction with the French dealer Durand-Ruel, another of the refugees, who had somehow managed to get 1,500 paintings out of France and had opened a gallery at 168 New Bond Street.

Daubigny's introduction was flatteringly complimentary: 'This is a young man who will be better than any of us.' But Durand-Ruel needed little persuasion. He already knew and liked Monet's work, and even had one of his pictures with him in London.

Durand-Ruel was forty when he first met Monet. A remarkable man, he had been forced to abandon an army career because of ill health, and had inherited from his father one of the first Paris art galleries, which specialized in the Fontainebleau painters and the Romantics. He learned the business inside out and, being ambitious, determined to try his hand with the contemporary generation of artists, among them Corot, Daumier, Courbet, Daubigny and Diaz, and most of the Barbizon school. As he himself opened more and more sumptuous galleries, he proceeded to raise the asking prices his painters could command by a simple but effective expedient. The trick was to send for auction the paintings he was interested in, and then push up the bidding in association with his colleagues. It was a manœuvre destined to enjoy great popularity in the future.

The encounter with Claude Monet was providential for both men. For some years Paul Durand-Ruel had been trying to attract new painters, the successors of the generation of 1830, and he was therefore delighted to meet a painter whose work he had already remarked. Through

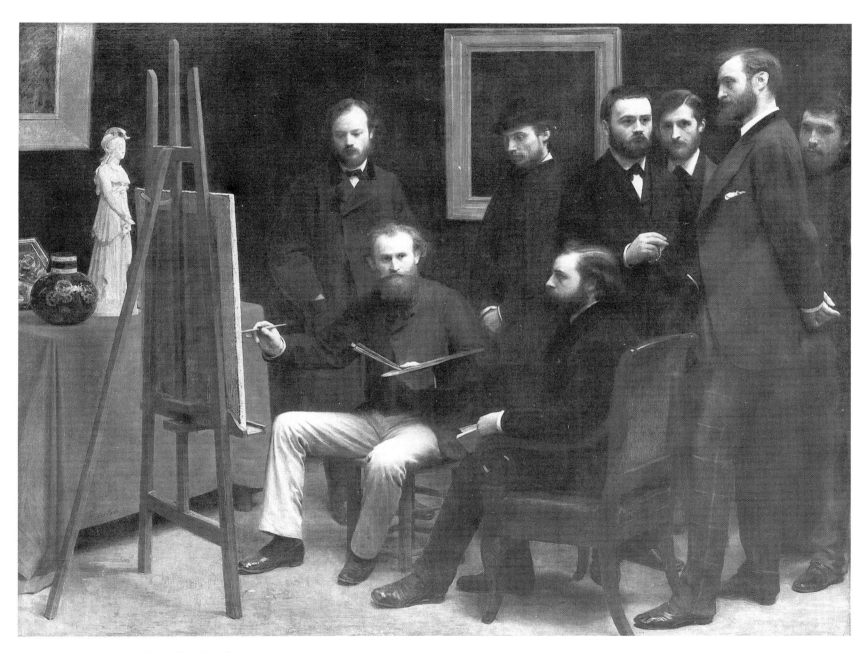

Fantin-Latour : Batignolles Studio, 1870.

him he was to make contact with the independent artists, the future Impressionists, first Pissarro, then Sisley, Manet, Degas and Renoir. As for Monet, it hardly needs stressing that the chance to sell his canvases for the modest but fair sum of 300 francs each was a stroke of unexpected good fortune. 'Durand was my salvation,' declared Monet at the height of his fame. Durand-Ruel's gamble was the more remarkable as he never sold a single painting by Monet in his London gallery. He hardly cared: he was passionate in his support for the Impressionists and remained so until the day he died, several times avoiding ruin in order to keep faith with the painters he loved.

Thanks to this new source of income Monet and his family were able to live in comfort in a furnished flat in Kensington, and Monet was free to throw himself into his work. He fell in love with London at once, and was especially fond of the embankment, the bridges, the leafy parks and the view of the Houses of Parliament through the mist. He never tired of painting these places, shrouded in their glowing grey haze, and in the course of his various visits to London produced more than a hundred paintings. In the company of his friend Pissarro he also visited the museums and galleries of the capital, paying particular attention to the Turners in the National Gallery. Contrary to popular belief, he did not receive any great enlightenment from these swirling compositions, full of dramatic effects of the light. Indeed he did not particularly like them and thought Turner melodramatic, criticizing the opacity of the shadows that made 'holes' in the canvas. It is nevertheless impossible not to be reminded of Turner when one sees Monet's *Rouen Cathedral* series, or his later views of Venice. One is forced to the conclusion that he must by then, more or less unconsciously, have assimilated Turner's influence into his own style.

Life in London would have been positively pleasant had it not been for the terrible news from France: the death of

the loyal Bazille in the battle of Beaune-la-Rolande; the death of Monet's father in January 71; the looting of Pissarro's house in Louveciennes by the Prussians; the establishment of the Commune.

It was only after the suppression of the popular uprising that Monet determined to return to France. If he went straight to Le Havre he knew he would be faced with settling his father's estate, small as it was, and he chose instead to play truant. By June 1871 he was in the small town of Zaandam in Holland, which he may have chosen because he had heard of it from Daubigny, who once worked in the area.

Like the period in London, his stay in Holland was hugely successful from an artistic point of view. Durand-Ruel's purchases freed him from all anxieties about money; he was able to visit Amsterdam and explore the museums, and bought in a grocer's shop a pile of Japanese prints, which he later hung in the dining room at Giverny. He was enchanted by the conventionally pretty countryside, the polders and windmills, the barges on the canals and above all the marvellous cloud-filled skies. 'There's a lifetime's painting here,' he wrote in delight to Pissarro. As always, he worked in a fever, accumulating dozens of landscapes in the five months he spent in the small town. He was so happy there that he went back three years later to paint the scenes he had not had time to record.

The golden age of Impressionism opens with Claude Monet's move to Argenteuil. Now it was Monet who played the role formerly held by Manet, as catalyst for the movement. With the exception of Degas, hostile to *plein air* painting, all the little group who used to meet at the Guerbois would go to Argenteuil to paint in the garden and work at Monet's side on the banks of the Seine. They were in total accord; even Manet, hitherto opposed to such practices, came and set up his easel by the waterside, and painted oarsmen and yachts, Monet in his studio boat, Camille sitting on the grass with Jean. These are the only paintings of his that can truly be called Impressionist.

Renoir again worked in close association with his old friend, as at the 'Grenouillère', and the empathy between them was so great that their paintings of the same motif are virtually indistinguishable. Pissarro and Sisley were frequent visitors, and even Cézanne, unsociable by nature, came to see what was happening. Later still Caillebotte became attached to the group.

It was shortly after returning from Holland that Monet moved to Argenteuil, guided in his choice of home by Manet, whose family owned a large estate at Genevilliers on the other side of the Seine. For Monet, obliged to see clients and dealers in Paris, it was important that there was an excellent rail link with the capital (precisely the reason why Argenteuil is today a dormitory-suburb of Paris, though it still retains something of its rural character). The house he rented from a lawyer's widow in November 71 was situated between the station and the river. It already had a studio, installed by the previous tenant Théodule Ribot, but the accommodation was far too cramped, and in October 74 the family moved to a house with a garden overlooking the Seine. The landlord was a carpenter who enjoyed the name of Adonis Flament.

The first two years in Argenteuil were happy in every respect. Camille blossomed and Jean grew into an appealing child—they appear together in Monet's delightful *Wild Poppies*. Thanks to Durand-Ruel and other collectors, money was plentiful. Increasingly there would be buyers eager to acquire the paintings executed in Holland and in Argenteuil, Rouen, Le Havre and Paris.

Monet, now in his thirties, was at the peak of his creative powers. In a mood of near euphoria, and with bewilder-

ing rapidity, he painted the masterpieces of the first part of his career. From the moment he arrived he set out to explore along the banks of the Seine, setting up his easel in Petit-Genevilliers, Asnières, Carrière-sur-Seine and Bougival. Often he painted spots virtually on his own doorstep, as with his two famous scenes of the road bridge and railway bridge at Argenteuil, and his various views of the Bassin, a sort of lake formed by a widening of the river, which was very popular with rowers and yachtsmen. Many of these canvases were painted from his studio boat, which he had bought as soon as he arrived in Argenteuil and had fitted with a tall cabin so that he could work in all weathers.

The paintings of this period, mostly from the motif, are characterized by a much more careful handling. True there are studies of charming spontaneity, painted in whiplash strokes, but also a large number of painstakingly 'finished' canvases. One feels that, although he denied it, Monet was responding to the criticisms from collectors that his works could be more polished. His preliminary drawing was now far more solid, the handling more meticulous, the canvas covered with little dabs of paint forming a fine iridescent grid that appeared almost alive.

This is very much the style of the paintings done on short trips to Rouen and Le Havre. Monet no longer had family in Le Havre but his brother Léon lived in Rouen, where he ran a chemical laboratory; he was one of Claude's most loyal supporters and bought several of his paintings.

Travelling a lot—a second trip to Holland in 1874—and working without a break, Monet still found time to keep up his old friendships. When he went to Paris he always visited La Nouvelle Athènes, the quiet café in the Place Pigalle that had replaced the Guerbois as a meeting-point. At one of these reunions an old idea of Bazille's was revived, to organize a group exhibition independent of the Salon. Over the weeks and months the plans were made,

Renoir : Portrait of Monet, 1872.

not without considerable dissension. Pissarro was fired with socialist ideals and would put forward wild propositions, which were then angrily countered by Degas, who believed it was essential to include a few establishment artists to lend the group credibility. He was outvoted by the rest, and in the end the only outsiders admitted were de Nittis, Bracquemond, Lépine, Ottin and Latouche. Early in 1874 the 'Société anonyme coopérative d'artistes peintres, sculpteurs et graveurs' was formally established. Discussion then centred on organizing the exhibition itself. The linchpin of the enterprise was Renoir, ably assisted by Degas, who had decided to cooperate after all. Manet was fearful of offending the influential academic painters on the Salon jury and remained in the background, a decision supported by Fantin-Latour. The 'hacks' were unimpressed by this evidence of his restraint and continued to make him wait for the medal he coveted.

The exhibition opened on 15 April at 35 boulevard des Capucines, in rooms made available by the photographer Nadar. This astonishing man was also a cartoonist and successful caricaturist, a journalist and writer, and a balloonist. He was a regular attender at the group's gatherings and enlivened their debates with his fiery outbursts. He generously lent his luxurious suite of rooms, the red velvet on the walls supplying a sumptuous background for the 165 paintings submitted by 30 contributors. Among these were *La Loge* and a *Dancer* by Renoir, Cézanne's *Modern Olympia* and *The House of the Hanged Man*, Degas' *Ballet Examination* and Monet's *Impression: Sunrise*.

The art world flocked to see this public defiance of the Beaux-Arts painters, now more firmly entrenched than ever in their position of superiority. The crowds attending the opening erupted in shock, anger and mirth, barely pausing to examine the pictures. As always happens, there was one particular critic more interested in dis-

playing his own wit than in giving an account of the paintings. This was Louis Leroy, who wrote a famous—or infamous—article in *Charivari*, a satirical magazine of the day. His main target was a study by Claude Monet, executed 'outside the harbour at Le Havre a year ago and christened rather haphazardly *Impression: Sunrise*'. He went on to categorize all the artists as 'impressionists', which he intended as a term of abuse—having no idea that 'impression' was a description previously used by, for example, Huet, who entitled one of his pictures *Impression: Seascape*. Leroy could not know that the painters he intended to denigrate would take up the name and make Impressionism into the most famous movement in modern French art history.

There were other critical articles of much greater intelligence by Castagnary, Philippe Burty and A. Sylvestre, but these were forgotten in the scandal. The exhibition was well attended but, alas, did not make a profit. The money received in entrance fees did not cover the costs of organization. And there were fewer sales than the artists had hoped. Monet exhibited nine pictures and was luckier than most in selling one of them, *Impression: Sunrise*, to a collector who was to play an important role in his life, Ernest Hoschedé.

One of the reasons why the group was prompted to set up an exhibition in the first place was that Durand-Ruel no longer supplied an outlet for their work. Monet and Degas were particularly hard hit as he had bought from them regularly even though he sold very little. Durand-Ruel was a casualty of the economic crisis in which France was plunged at the end of 1873, in consequence of the defeat of 1870. The painters had no choice but to look for other commercial possibilities, and for Monet that need was urgent as he had spent all he earned and had no savings. He kept detailed accounts and we know from his record books his precise income in these years: in 1872,

12,000 francs, plus 6,000 francs from the legacy left by Camille's father; in 1873, 24,000 francs; in 1874, 10,554 francs; in 1875, 9,765 francs; in 1876, 12,313 francs; in 1877, 15,197 francs.

In those non-inflationary times, a doctor in a good area could afford to employ two servants and hire a carriage to make his visits on an income not in excess of 10,000 francs a year. On the face of it, there seems no reason why Monet should have been always asking for money and sending desperate appeals to Manet, Zola and Caillebotte. The truth is, if he was financially stretched and sometimes even in real need, it was because he allowed money to slip through his fingers—he always lived up to and beyond his means. While Pissarro's family were potatoes, the Monets employed two servants, a nursemaid for Jean and a gardener. They ate lavishly and well, drank the best cognac and ordered fine wine by the barrel from Bordeaux. Camille would pose for her husband in ravishing and expensive ensembles.

Ernest Hoschedé had bought several other canvases as well as *Impression: Sunrise*, and for a time Monet hoped he would take the place of Durand-Ruel. But alas, the financier was already on the brink of ruin when he invited Monet to spend a few weeks at his château in Montgeron, with a commission to decorate the salon. Hoschedé had inherited a thriving business from his father, and the château was the dowry brought by his wife Alice Ringo, who came from a wealthy and well-connected family. But his passion for collecting led him to neglect his business affairs, to quite disastrous effect. Over a period of a few years he had assembled a magnificent collection of the works of Manet, Boudin, Pissarro, Monet, Degas and Sisley. Early in 1874 he was forced to put more than one hundred paintings up for auction, in an attempt to recoup some of his losses, but his mania for collecting reasserted itself and he immediately used the proceeds to buy more.

By 1876, when he entertained Monet, he was a declared bankrupt, and when his collection was sold in the following year 117 Impressionist paintings came onto the market, among them 16 by Monet. A last desperate attempt to salvage something from the wreckage was unsuccessful. He and his family were ruined.

While Monet was staying at Montgeron he painted four panels for the salon, among them the famous *White Turkeys*, influenced in its composition by Japanese prints. Ernest Hoschedé was in Paris a lot of the time, trying to rescue his fortunes, and Monet frequently found himself alone with his young wife Alice. She confided her feelings to him and found a sympathetic listener. Perhaps it was in the course of one of these conversations that they became emotionally attached, for certainly a relationship started between them that was more than friendship and was to develop into an enduring bond.

Monet left Montgeron at the end of the summer but did not remain long in Argenteuil. That autumn he asked permission of the railway company to paint in the confines of the Gare Saint-Lazare. He had evidently not forgotten those conversations in the café about modern life being the subject of art, a notion first expressed by Baudelaire and popularized by Goncourt and Duranty. The station attracted him as a subject because of its smoke-filled atmosphere, suffused with light pouring in through the glass roof. Working in concentrated bursts, he completed the series based on the *Gare Saint-Lazare* in 1878.

Some of the paintings of this series were included in the third Impressionist exhibition of 1877. Émile Zola was in ecstasies at seeing his dream become a reality, and wrote in a Marseille paper: 'This year Monet has exhibited some superb interiors of stations. In them you can hear the trains grinding to a halt, you can see the swirls of smoke spreading through these vast sheds. That is where paint-

Manet : Monet in his Studio, 1874.

ing has arrived at today... Our artists should discover the poetry of stations, just as their fathers before them discovered the poetry of forests and rivers.' At the Impressionist exhibitions of 1876 and 1877, Monet was approached by a number of collectors interested in his work, among them: Dr de Bellio, Charles Ephrusi (editor of the *Gazette des Beaux-Arts*), Victor Choquet, Zacharie Astruc, Charles Deudon (an acquaintance of Renoir), Henri Rouart (a painter himself and a friend of Degas), Ernest May (a stockbroker), Emmanuel Chabrier (who owned *The Bar at the Folies-Bergère*), the tenor Fauré (an avid collector who became the owner of 67 Manets and almost as many Monets), the celebrated writer Alphonse Daudet, and Dr Gachet, friend of Cézanne and Pissarro and later van Gogh's patron.

The list is incomplete, but serves to show that, even with the enforced withdrawal of Durand-Ruel, there was never a time when people were not interested in Monet's paintings. However, the prices they were prepared to pay were lower than those that prevailed just after Monet's return from England. Often a canvas would make no more than 200 francs. In 1878 Dr de Bellio paid only 210 francs for *Impression: Sunrise*, although Hoschedé had bought it four years earlier for 800 francs.

The 'business side' was getting to be more and more of a headache, and the unfortunate Monet wrote letter after letter in the effort to place his paintings or to borrow from friends. Caillebotte, Dr de Bellio, Manet and Zola were all regular recipients of such missives. By late 1877, Monet was at his wits' end and was obliged to make a hasty departure from Argenteuil, leaving as security for his landlord Adonis Flament, to whom he owed rent, the vast canvas of *Le Déjeuner sur l'herbe*. He did not recover the picture until seven years later, by which time it was in a deplorable condition. He was obliged to cut away the parts that were rotten.

Monet owed money everywhere, to the man who sold him his materials, the baker, the butcher, even to a painter and decorator called Charles Braque, who by chance had a son called Georges...

The three years Monet lived in Vétheuil were marked by grief and poverty. He was probably at his lowest ebb in both his public and personal life.

After spending a few months in Paris at his *pied-à-terre* in the rue d'Edimbourg (when he painted *The Rue Montorgueil Decked Out with Flags*), he moved with his family, in September 1878, to this little village some sixty kilometres from Paris, in an area he had always loved. With help from Manet he was able to rent a large house with what then passed for 'all modern comforts', running water at the kitchen sink and proper flush lavatories—details recounted admiringly by a journalist who came to interview him. A large house was vital since his own family had now joined forces with the Hoschedé household, which consisted of two adults and six children. The château at Montgeron had been sold the previous year by the receiver and Ernest Hoschedé had accepted Monet's offer of hospitality with gratitude. Since Hoschedé could make very little in the way of a contribution, Monet found himself responsible for twelve people, plus two servants and a governess. In practice Alice's husband was rarely there. Possibly he knew quite well that Monet had replaced him in his wife's affections, for he was aware of her resentment at the loss of the château that had been her dowry. Or perhaps his absence was due more to the interest of his new career as an art critic, in which he felt he had at last found his vocation. For thirteen years Monet and Alice were to maintain a façade, always addressing each other in public as Monsieur and Madame—and retaining the formality even when they exchanged letters.

Manet : The Monet Family in their Garden, 1874.

The Giverny Garden.

This farcical situation turned to tragedy when Camille was discovered to have cancer of the uterus. She had been unwell since the birth of her second son, Michel, in March 78, she was badly served by a country doctor, and died on 3 September 79 at the age of thirty-two. Alice Hoschedé nursed her with devotion and was at her side to the last. Monet's behaviour at the time of Camille's death was extraordinary—and revealing. Struck by the look of his dead wife's face under its veil, he took up his brushes and painted, in long sweeping strokes, a sort of Ophelia-figure drowning in mauve net. Only later did he realize just how odd his reaction had been, and wrote to Georges Clemenceau describing what happened: 'I found myself with my eyes riveted on those tragic temples, in the act of searching quite mechanically for the precise sequence, the advance of the changes imposed on the pallor of her features by death. Tones of blue, yellow, grey, what am I to say? That is the point I had reached…'

On the same day he wrote an emotional letter to Dr de Bellio: 'My poor wife passed away this morning at half past ten, after terrible suffering. I am distraught to find myself alone with my poor children. Once again I ask a favour of you, to take out of pawn the medallion for which I enclose the ticket. It is the only souvenir of the past my wife was able to keep, and I want to be able to put it round her neck before she goes.'

Life then began to return to something like normality, and the dead woman was forgotten, so completely forgotten that no one bothered to see her grave was maintained, neither Claude nor Alice nor Camille's sons. In 1966, as an act of piety, the Vétheuil council located the tomb and paid for its restoration. It is the more surprising to learn that Monet always kept in his room the portrait of his dead wife—something that must have taken a degree of courage as Alice demanded that everything connected with Camille should be destroyed.

No sooner was the funeral over than Monet's creditors descended in a pack. Furious at being put off yet again they made scenes that terrified the children. One poured the contents of a vase of flowers into the piano, the laundrywoman refused to return the sheets, and they could not even write letters begging for help as the postwoman refused to continue giving them stamps on credit!

In that winter of 79-80 there was no wood or coal for heating, and it was the coldest winter of the century. On 10 December, in Paris, the temperature was recorded as minus 25° and the ice on the Seine was 30 cm thick. During the night of 5 January the inhabitants of Vétheuil were awakened by a noise like gunfire: the sound of the ice breaking up. The next morning Monet braved the cold, in a fever to set down on canvas the phenomenon that had occurred. For several days he did nothing but paint landscapes of icefloes and fog over the Seine, producing a series of canvases that represent a turning-point in his *oeuvre*. On this occasion he was not evoking a scene carefully selected for its charm and beauty, he was painting what presented itself to him, almost an abstraction, the effect of light striking objects, the transmutation of colour in the thick atmosphere. There was nothing remotely picturesque about it. Returning to the earlier manner of *Impression: Sunrise*, he worked swiftly and under tension, almost schematically, applying the pigment in strokes, slashing and dotting the canvas in a glinting mosaic. Sometimes he would use a sort of wash, as though painting a watercolour, creating vast shimmering expanses, adapting his technique always to the effect he wanted to create. His works from this period were exhibited on 7 June 1880 at the La Vie Moderne gallery, on the boulevard des Italiens; the gallery was owned by Charpentier, the publisher, and run by Edmond Renoir, younger brother of the painter. Monet's pictures were received with delight, both by the press and the afficionados of the art world. His reputation was beginning to rise. Several of the landscapes were sold and the money was enough to relieve Monet of the worst of the pressure. That year he took his extended family to spend a relaxed holiday at Petites-Dalles, near Fécamp, where his brother Léon had a villa. Over the next twenty years he was to return to the area again and again at different times of the year.

The success of this exhibition had the effect of setting Monet further apart from the rest of the group. The previous year he had not bothered to attend the fourth Impressionist exhibition, even though it included 29 of his canvases. In 1880 he was too busy with the preparations for his first one-man show, and did not contribute. His colleagues were the more shocked to discover that, for the first time in ten years, he had submitted a painting to the Salon. And, what is more, it was accepted. Unhappily for Monet, his fine landscape of Lavacourt, one of his more 'polished' works, was hung so high on a wall that no one could see it. But his defection, followed by Renoir's departure, signalled the beginning of the end of Impressionism as a concerted movement. The two friends took part in the group exhibition of 1883, but after that all of them went their separate ways.

For Monet there was now every reason to be optimistic. The influential dealer Georges Petit had begun to buy his works, and in February 81 Paul Durand-Ruel, temporarily out of the wood, purchased 15 canvases for 300 francs each. Monet's account books tell the story. In the terrible year of 1879 he earned only 12,258 francs, as compared with 20,400 francs in 1881. The days of penury were behind him, and though he pleaded poverty it was a gross exaggeration of his difficulties.

Monet's sense of relief is palpable in the dazzling picture he created in the autumn of 1881 as a farewell to Vétheuil. *Monet's Garden in Vétheuil* shows a riot of sunflowers and other plants, in the midst of which appear the two figures of his son, Michel, and the youngest Hoschedé boy, Jean. The brilliant light that floods over them could truly be said to be the light of happiness.

The decade following Monet's departure from Vétheuil is notable in three main respects: for his painting of 'series', the move to Giverny and, a new departure, his burgeoning friendships with a number of major writers.

Monet had been in his new home in Poissy for only a few weeks when he left again for a painting expedition to the Normandy coast. Dieppe, Varangeville, Pourville, Étretat, Fécamp—he never tired of painting the places he had first seen with a painter's eye in the company of Boudin, as a very young man. Moreover, he detested Poissy, which he had chosen only because Zola recommended it for his children's education. And it was as well to be out of the way should Ernest Hoschedé take it into his head to pay one of his rare visits to his family. Monet's domestic situation was fast becoming intolerable. Alice refused point-blank either to go back to her husband or to seek an official separation. The façade of bourgeois respectability fooled no one, and there were frequent scenes with Alice and the children. Torn between love and a desire to conform, Monet was extremely unhappy. His solution was simply to walk away from the problem. In that first summer following the move to Poissy, he spent most of the time in Pourville, near Dieppe, where he had found an inn he liked, and even arranged for Alice and the children to join him there for their holidays.

He might have been happier if he could have found gratification in his work, but the letters he wrote to Alice ('Chère Madame'), and to Durand-Ruel and Pissarro after his return to Poissy, are nothing but a string of complaints. The weather, the sea, the tides, all were against him, and what was worst, he thought he had 'lost his touch'.

He destroyed or scratched out a large percentage of what he produced.

Even now his financial situation was not completely secure. In January 82 he learned that the bank who had loaned money to Durand-Ruel had failed, and its director had been arrested. The unfortunate dealer found himself in an impossible situation. Unless he could increase the volume of his sales, he would be unable to repay the loans. Monet was in trepidation. Would it be Vétheuil all over again? Happily this was not the case. Durand-Ruel was courageous and loyal to a fault, and he continued to buy Monet's paintings.

As a means of raising money, he suggested to the Impressionists that he should organize another group exhibition of their work. All were agreeable, except Cézanne and Degas. Monet was not enthusiastic but made no objection once he knew that Degas had withdrawn. There was no love lost between them, and the great painter of dancers and cafés once declared he would like to have the *plein-air* artists shot.

Monet's twenty-nine canvases made up the largest single contribution. But his heart was not in the enterprise, and it was the last time he exhibited with his old friends from the Guerbois days. This seventh Impressionist exhibition opened on May 1 at 25 rue du Faubourg-Saint-Honoré, but it was not the success Durand-Ruel had hoped. The general public had ceased to regard these painters as a novelty and only the true connoisseurs bothered to attend. Even they bought very little. The press too had tired of the subject and found little new to say. But it is worth noting that an old adversary, Albert Wolf, decided the time had come to revise his opinions.

The major event of these years was the move to Giverny. Walking by the Seine one spring day, looking for motifs, Monet had been enraptured by the sight of a frothy white veil of apple blossom covering a little village at the confluence of the Seine and the Epte. There happened to be a simple cottage to let, a long, low building, and without even consulting Alice, he rented it. Today, with its irregular flights of steps and various studios and greenhouses, it is impossible to imagine the original primitive dwelling.

It was not until he bought the property, in 1892, that Monet was able to start to improve and enlarge it, as money became available, making it an agreeable home.

In any case, Monet was less interested in the building itself than in the land that went with it. He cut down part of the adjacent orchard to clear a space for a garden, not a grandiose affair, just a plot with paths crossing at right angles. The yew trees lining the path from the gate gave the house a dark and unwelcoming aspect, and these were first cut back and then replaced with metal pergolas covered with roses and clematis. The lawns were edged with borders of irises and dotted with beds of peonies. It would take a whole book (such as the one Clemenceau wrote) to describe this garden in full. Suffice to say that it was not at all ornate, in the fashion favoured by the nineteenth century, but was filled with ordinary cottage-garden flowers, clumped together in brilliant displays. It was made by a painter to supply him with themes for his pictures.

But Monet did not linger at Giverny, any more than he had been content to remain in Poissy. The moment his family was settled he left for Paris, to attend Manet's funeral, and then spent the whole of the summer and autumn in Étretat. Although permanently dissatisfied with what he produced, he worked happily and energetically, painting several views of the famous cliffs. He enjoyed the solitude of the small resort in the low season, and after a day in the wind and rain was quite content to smoke a pipe and drink a glass of calvados. Even two or three glasses. His happiness was completed when, in 1885, he chanced to meet Guy de Maupassant, who often retreated to his villa in Étretat to write. He vastly enjoyed his conversations with this gifted man who was so utterly different from himself. They had in common a love of the Normandy coast, and Maupassant spoke with wonderful eloquence; he could always find the words to express his admiration for the canvases Monet showed him.

This decade was marked by a series of fortuitous meetings and new friendships, particularly important for Monet because he led such a secluded life, either hidden away in Giverny or on one of his solitary expeditions. Through Durand-Ruel he had been introduced to Octave Mirbeau, who proved to be a passionate gardener and also an admirer of his work, about which he subsequently wrote with considerable insight. The two men became close friends when Monet stayed with Mirbeau in Noirmoutier in November 1886. Shortly before that, Monet had met the art critic Gustave Geffroy, in a chance encounter at the inn in Belle-Ile. Not only were the two destined to become lifelong friends, Geffroy wrote for the immensely prestigious *La Justice* and it turned out that he had the highest regard for Monet's work. Over the years he published numerous articles and studies on Monet's painting, and also a full biography. He was too the means of reuniting the artist with an old friend, Georges Clemenceau, a medical student when Monet had known him in 1863. Clemenceau took upon himself the task of acting as a sort of publicist for Monet's work, and he also supported him in his old age after Alice's death, when he was afflicted by feelings of despair.

1883 saw Claude Monet venturing further afield. In December, together with Renoir, he made a short trip to what was then known as the Riviera, getting as far as Genoa. He was enthralled by the look of the landscape but did not communicate his enthusiasm to his friend, whose presence he found inhibiting. In the new year he set off alone for Bordighera and Menton, where he worked in a state of euphoria, revelling in the natural splendours and the mauve haze that enveloped the landscape. 'It's going to be rather painful for people who can't stand blue and pink, because it's precisely that brilliance, that enchanted light that I'm trying to catch, and anyone who hasn't visited this part of the world will, I'm sure, believe I've invented it, although actually I'm underplaying the tonal intensity: everything is the blue of a pigeon's neck or the colour of flaming punch.' He left Bordighera at the end of April with fifty canvases, expressing his thanks to Monsieur Moreno, who had made his stay so pleasant, by presenting him with the gift of a large apple. It was a not untypical gesture.

When the landscapes were exhibited by Durand-Ruel they were greeted with universal acclaim. The critics accepted defeat gracefully, and the Maître de Giverny was the new name on everyone's lips. It did Monet no harm at all that, although he had not deserted Durand-Ruel, he was also on the books of Georges Petit, whose gallery in the rue de Sèze was frequented by fashionable society. It might be legitimate to pour scorn on unknown artists, but it was another matter with a painter who was shown at the most exclusive gallery of them all.

Practical to the last, Monet used the rivalry between the two dealers to good effect, letting them compete with each other to offer the highest price. A little later he also introduced into his machinations Théo van Gogh, who ran Goupil's avant-garde gallery, and Gaston Bernheim. The result was that canvases for which he had been happy to receive 300 francs in 1881 were selling, ten years later, for 2,500 francs, and by 1885 had reached 12,000 francs.

At the end of December, Monet paid a short visit to Holland and then spent some months in Belle-Ile, two important periods from an artistic point of view as they show him experimenting with stronger, almost violent

Monet in his House at Giverny
with the Duke of Trevise.

colour. From a ten-day trip to The Hague, in spring 1886, he returned with five brilliant canvases expressing his dazzled reaction to the tulip fields, 'enough to drive a poor painter mad'. One can see why the Fauves claimed Monet as one of their own, and why Marcel Proust devoted a whole column in *Le Figaro* to the experience of seeing one of these paintings.

The Belle-Ile pictures continued in the same vein. From September to the end of November 1886, Monet produced 39 canvases, among the most powerful he ever painted. Here were no delicately swirling mists, no gleaming waters, just a crystalline light flooding over a landscape of rocks and white-crested waves. Monet practically ignored the sky, concentrating on the basalt rocks lashed by the sea's fury. 'I'm really excited,' he wrote to Caillebotte, 'in spite of the difficulties, because I've been used to painting the Channel, and of course I had my way of doing things, whereas the ocean is quite different.' When Geffroy accompanied him to the 'wild coast', he was forcibly struck by the painter's mood of exaltation. 'Claude Monet works in the wind and the rain,' he wrote in his book. 'He has to dress like the fishermen here, in boots, swathed in jerseys, enveloped in an oilskin with a hood. Sometimes the gusts of wind tear palette and brushes out of his hands. His easel is lashed down with ropes and weighted with stones. The painter stands firm and launches into his composition as if into battle.'

Before he left Giverny for Belle-Ile, Monet had received a copy of Zola's novel *L'Œuvre*, with a friendly dedication. Contrary to some reports, he was not taken by surprise at what he read, and nor were Cézanne and the other Impressionists: the novel had already appeared in serial form in *Gil Blas*. But, if not surprised, Monet was certainly not indifferent. He thought there was too much of a parallel between certain episodes in his own life and those described by Zola in the book. The fact that the un-fortunate hero Claude Lantier had the same Christian name lent a spurious note of authenticity to the events that took place. And Lantier's suicide and his behaviour in front of the body of his dead son came uncomfortably close to his own attempted suicide and the death of Camille.

He wrote a brief and dignified note to Zola acknowledging receipt of the book, but the hurt is evident, the more so as he was fond of Zola. 'You have taken care, deliberately, that no character of yours resembles any one of us, but in spite of that I fear that among the press and public alike, our enemies will pronounce the name of Monet, all our names, to prove us failures. It was not any part of your intentions, that I cannot believe... but I have struggled for so long and I fear that, just as I have arrived, our enemies will use this book to destroy us.'

The two men were not properly reconciled until the Dreyfus affair, on which their views coincided. When Zola published his open letter 'J'accuse' in 1898, for which he received a term of imprisonment, Monet gave him his unqualified support.

In 1890 Claude Monet embarked upon the most personal and distinctive of his works, those which mark him out as one of the great painters of his age.

The major series of *Haystacks, Poplars, Rouen Cathedral*, and later the *Waterlilies*, were in many ways a logical development of his existing working methods. He had often in the past chosen to concentrate on a particular motif or set of motifs: one thinks in particular of the products of his first visit to London, the group of landscapes executed in Antibes and Juan-les-Pins in the winter of 1888, the twenty Japanese-influenced studies he brought back from Norway, and indeed of the homogeneity of the works he produced on his many subsequent visits to London. He had grown to love the city when he lived there in 1870, fascinated by the quality of the light diffused through the fog. Up to 1904, scarcely a year passed without his returning there. From a hotel room overlooking the Thames, or down by the river, he painted Waterloo and Charing Cross bridges and the Houses of Parliament, using that intense, animated style that links him so firmly to Fauvism. It is worth remembering that it was as a direct result of seeing these pictures in Durand-Ruel's gallery that Vlaminck and Derain decided to go to London themselves and paint exactly these subjects. For Monet there was an additional motive in going to England, as it gave him the chance to see old and valued friends such as Whistler, who moved in influential circles and gained admission for his friend to the Royal Society of British Artists, and Sargent, who was always flattering in his praises.

The paintings from Antibes, like the Bordighera pictures, are symphonies of blue, mauve and pink. When Théo van Gogh showed ten of these canvases at the Goupil gallery they were given an ecstatic reception by Maupassant, Mirbeau, Mallarmé and Geffroy. Be it said that Monet took care to present his more influential friends with the occasional painting, as an inducement to loyalty; an apple would scarcely have sufficed in their case.

The Creuse is a harsh and wild stretch of countryside, and one may wonder why Monet chose to spend three months there early in 1899. Yet he liked Fresselines, where he was warmly welcomed by the poet Maurice Rollinat. Only the rapidity of the change from winter snow to spring growth caused him anguish. In order to finish one winter canvas he actually hired a peasant to strip a tree of all its fresh green leaves. The unfortunate Rollinat was another recipient of apples from Monet—he received a basketful as thanks for his hospitality over the three months.

Clemenceau enthused over the forceful style of these Creuse paintings, and in his delight Monet forgot himself so far as to make him a present of one of them, a view of the Bloc, a stark rock formation dominating the landscape,

done in a spare, brutal style of which Jean Dubuffet would not have been ashamed. Today it is in the collection of the Queen of England.

The visit to Norway came five years later. Monet's motive for the trip was quite simply the chance it offered to paint unsullied snow that did not melt away at the first hint of a thaw. For two months he stayed in Oslo with the wife of the dramatist Bjornson, a rival of Ibsen and a future Nobel Prize winner. He relished the dry, sunny climate and would set out happily, wrapped in a bearskin, hands encased in gloves and beard dripping with icicles, to paint for hours in temperatures of minus 25°.

The years that preceded the painting of the great series were happy and successful, and enlivened by new friends and activities. Monet was relatively indifferent to the honour accorded him when three of his works were shown at the International Exhibition of 1899. True, it represented his final triumph over the old establishment, but he was far more concerned with his joint exhibition with Rodin, which was being organized by Georges Petit. To have a panorama of his own work from 1865 onwards presented in conjunction with *The Burghers of Calais*, a masterpiece by the colossus of French art, known the world over, that truly was an honour. He was disappointed when the exhibition enjoyed no more than a modest success.

Happily his finances were in a good state and, thanks to the activities of Théo van Gogh, Georges Petit and Durand-Ruel, there was always a steady stream of new collectors coming to join the ranks of the old. Some of these were American, as Durand-Ruel had opened a gallery in New York in 1886. At first Monet had not liked the idea of losing his work to the 'Yankees', but the New York papers seemed to appreciate him and the financial rewards were considerable, and so he raised no further objections.

The early 1890s were marked by the deaths of two people important to him in very different ways. First came the demise of Ernest Hoschedé in 1891, and three years later the loss of his good and loyal friend Caillebotte. Alice had behaved impeccably during the last months of her husband's illness, returning to the family home to be with him. The prodigal collector was buried with all due pomp and circumstance, and today all three of them are at rest under the same stone in the cemetery at Giverny: Ernest, Alice and Claude.

Nine months later, in July 1882, Alice and Claude Monet were married in a civil and religious ceremony. At last they were able to cease addressing each other in public as Monsieur and Madame. For Monet this relieved much of the pressure, especially as Alice could no longer hold over his head the threat of returning to her husband if she was feeling jealous or aggrieved.

Caillebotte bequeathed his magnificent collection to the state, an act of generosity that aroused resistance in the establishment. It was to be their last stand. Renoir was the executor of Caillebotte's will and it was therefore his task to see that the legacy was accepted. He met with so many deliberate obstructions and delays that in the end he was forced to accept a compromise. A percentage only of the paintings would pass to the state, among them 6 Monets out of the original 16. Monet was frankly thrilled, since he was allowed to choose the canvases he regarded as his best.

There was a comparable campaign going on at that time, to buy Manet's *Olympia* for the Louvre. Monet was the prime mover in the enterprise and spent much of 1890 writing letters and raising the 20,000 francs for the purchase price. He was surprised to meet with a refusal from Zola, Mary Cassatt and Antonin Proust, a lifelong friend of Manet—with whom he nearly fought a duel—but he succeeded in reaching the target and Clemenceau was able to ensure that the gift was accepted.

Although greatly preoccupied with this philanthropic cause, Monet also started work on the *Haystacks* series—his first attempt to explore a single motif systematically, viewing it always from the same angle. The series of twenty canvases was almost immediately followed by another, the *Poplars*. Here again his aim was to study the transient effects of the light at different times of the day and different seasons of the year. Juggling with as many as ten canvases at once, in order to use his time economically, he would work on one to capture a particular effect that might last for only a few minutes, then move on to the next. Perhaps it was a sign of his advancing years that he chose two subjects within easy walking distance of his home in Giverny.

The *Haystacks* were hugely successful when they were exhibited by Goupil (now Boussod et Valadon) and Durand-Ruel. Pissarro, whose affection for Monet had always been tinged with an edge of friendly sarcasm, was on this occasion magnanimous: 'I thought it was most luminous and most masterly,' he wrote to his son Lucien, 'it's unanswerable.' When Mallarmé received one of the landscapes as a gift, he wrote in delight: 'Recently you dazzled me with your haystacks, Monet, so that I find myself looking at the fields through the memory of your painting; or rather, they insist on being seen so...' It would be nice to think that this elegantly phrased note was the one that arrived in an envelope still preserved at Giverny. It was addressed to:

Monsieur Monet que l'hiver ni
L'été sa vision ne leurre
Habite, en peignant Giverny
Sis auprès de Vernon dans l'Eure.

(Monsieur Monet, may neither winter/nor summer blur his vision,/lives, painting, in Giverny/situated in Vernon in the Eure.)

The *Poplars* aroused the same overwhelming response, summed up by Pissarro in his letter of congratulation:

'What a beautiful thing, the three compositions of poplars in the evening, how painterly they are, and how decorative!'

And so we arrive, logically, at the series based on *Rouen Cathedral*, which occupied much of 1892-93. The fifty canvases were painted in the course of two visits to Rouen, from the vantage point of the first-floor windows of houses facing the main entrance of the cathedral. Never had Monet been so depressed and discouraged. 'The more I go on, the more difficulty I have in conveying what I feel,' he wrote to Geffroy, 'and I tell myself, anyone who says he has finished a canvas is just boasting.' He exhausted himself in the effort of capturing the effects of light on the old stone, to the point where he simply abandoned everything, returned to Giverny and retired to bed. He so loathed the thought of what he had done that he waited a full month before he was able to open the cases in which the pictures were packed.

Most of these pictures are painted in a technique absolutely different from anything Monet had tried before. Where in the past he had normally applied the paint in distinct, divided dabs, now he superimposed the touches of pigment so that they formed an encrustation of colour. When you view the canvases from close to, they look grainy, a senseless jumble. But as you move further away, everything swims into focus. As with the earlier series, the motif is represented at different times of the day, and in different weathers, ranging from the mist of early morning to the full glare of the midday sun.

It was shortly after Monet's return from Norway, in May 95, that Durand-Ruel put on show twenty of the *Rouen Cathedral* sequence. They were, quite simply, a revelation. Artists and connoisseurs alike were united in praising his radical new perception and inspired technique. Cézanne, Renoir, Pissarro, even Degas, all were dumbfounded. Only the young 'divisionists', Signac,

Cross and Luce, had reservations. Georges Clemenceau published an ecstatic article in *La Justice*—indeed in his enthusiasm his style became so convoluted and flowery as to be well-nigh incomprehensible!

The only cloud was the reaction from Zola. In a column in *Le Figaro* he wrote, ambiguously: 'What I once supported, I shall continue to support', but went on to express many doubts and qualifications, and to regret that Impressionism had not produced 'its Ingres, its Delacroix or its Courbet'.

Monet by this time was practically oblivious to praise or attack. All that occupied his mind was the progress in digging out the pool for his water garden. It was to be the focus of his attentions for the remaining third of his life.

It was in November 1918, after the signing of the armistice with Germany, that Monet finally decided to donate to the French state the 19 *Waterlilies* panels housed in his specially constructed studio at Giverny. Up until then, despite repeated appeals from Clemenceau, he had refused to commit himself. It was not that he was against the idea in principle, simply that he could never accept the panels were finished, and would keep reworking them. In the event it was not until 12 April 1922, three years later, that he signed the formal deed of gift. Even then the paintings remained in Giverny until after his death, although he had approved the plans for their installation at the Orangerie in the Tuileries Gardens.

These two ensembles, each 40 metres in circumference, were the culmination of a process that started as Monet contemplated his lily pond as far back as 1897—indeed the gestation of the idea may go back even to the time when he first decided to buy a piece of marshland and chose to stock the pond with Nymphea, a particularly large and showy variety of waterlily. At all events, for about thirty years Monet made that lily pond the focus of his attentions, studying the effects of transparency in the water and the way it rippled and shimmered. Of course there were other concerns in his life—he made several visits to London, spent two months in Venice and also went to Spain with Alice in 1908—but he was obsessed with his *Waterlilies* project and spent every moment he could by the pond.

There is an early series of paintings that shows the pool itself, with its weeping willows, the flowers growing on the banks and the Japanese bridge hung with wistaria. It was seeing ten canvases of the series, exhibited by Durand-Ruel in 1900, that made Degas say to Monet, in reconciliation: 'They are not bad, your cups of camomile tea!'

The huge success enjoyed by the exhibition, and also a second held in 1909, was probably due not only to the originality of Monet's approach to his theme, but also to the fact that waterlilies, irises and agapanthus were all elements regularly used as decorative motifs in the Art Nouveau style currently in vogue.

Monet's second series was even more striking. Now there was no bridge, no plants, no trees, nothing identifiable to focus the eye. Even the sky was suggested only by its reflection in the water. The spectator was simply faced with a vast coloured surface.

These paintings and the ones that followed—236 in all—were generally painted from the motif, and Monet used them for reference in the creation of his 19 decorative panels, each 4 metres × 2 metres. He apparently told Roger-Marx in 1909 that he had an idea: 'For using the waterlilies theme for the decoration of a salon: carried along the walls, enclosing all the panels within its unity, I would

have provided the illusion of an endless whole, water with no horizon or bank... and to anyone who lived there, this room would have offered a refuge for peaceful meditation in the middle of an aquarium of flowers.'

All the essentials of the idea were there, but he delayed putting it into practice. The more so as the death of his wife Alice, in 1911, was followed by the loss of his son Jean in 1914. In his grief he spoke of giving up painting for ever, and Clemenceau needed all his powers of persuasion to make him return to work. Only then did he embark on the task. First he had a huge studio built, with a glass roof, and the panels were placed along the walls. After that he worked with surprising speed. Visited by the dealer René Gimpel in November 1918, he gave the following account of his working methods: 'All day long I work on these canvases. They are brought to me one after the other. In the atmosphere a colour reappears that I found the previous day and sketched in on one of the canvases. Someone quickly passes me that picture and as far as possible I try to fix that vision definitively, but in general it disappears as rapidly as it arrives, and gives way to another colour already set down a few days before on yet another study, which is instantly placed before me... and so it goes on all day!'

Gimpel gives a detailed account of his visit, and he mentions that Monet's son Michel and stepdaughter Blanche were quite perturbed at the way the elderly painter was constantly revising what he had done. His sight was deteriorating rapidly and they feared he was spoiling all he had achieved. Cataracts had begun to form over his eyes in 1908 and the changes in him had become quite marked.

Georges Clemenceau and Claude Monet.

Monet on his 80th Birthday painting Waterlilies.

A look at the paintings of this period, housed in the Musée Marmottan, shows that all suggestion of construction has disappeared, leaving coloured masses in yellows and oranges—the overall effect oddly reminiscent of 'gestural' painting.

In 1923 Monet bowed to pressure from Clemenceau, who reminded him of his medical training, and consented to an operation.   With the aid of special glasses procured for him by the painter André Barbier, in July 1925 he was able to write to his benefactor: 'My sight is entirely restored.   I work as never before, am pleased with what I am doing, and if the new glasses are even better, then I ask nothing more than to live till I am a hundred.'

It was his swan song.   He was old and tired.   By the time he died on 6 December 1926, after a short illness, he was interested in nothing but his garden, which he looked on as his true masterpiece.

Alerted by telegram Clemenceau hastened to Giverny, 700 kilometres from where he lived in La Vendée.   He arrived as the body was being placed in its coffin.   Pushing aside the undertaker's men, in the act of drawing a black sheet over the corpse, he tore a flowered curtain from the window and laid it in place, crying, 'No black for Claude Monet!'

There could have been no better epitaph.

Monet in his Garden at Giverny.

This snow scene, dated 1865, must in fact have been executed during the winter of 1866-67, when Claude Monet was stranded in Honfleur without any money. His family had learned of his liaison with a young woman called Camille and had cut his allowance.

A few months before, Monet had been obliged to make a hasty departure from the house in Sèvres where he and Camille had set up home together. He owed several back payments in rent and the landlord was threatening to send in the bailiffs. Thirty years later, Monet claimed he had slashed two hundred canvases before he left, so that they could not be seized as assets. He may have embroidered the tale somewhat in the telling since he went on to assert that the canvases were taken in any case and were later patched up and sold off in bundles of fifty for thirty francs!

Unlike Renoir, who regarded snow as a scar on the landscape, Monet loved these frozen vistas, and that winter painted numerous views of the Trouville road under snow and of the area around the Ferme Saint-Siméon. The farm, which today is a comfortable country inn, was then run by an old peasant woman called Mère Toutain and her daughter. Mère Toutain was a wonderful cook who delighted in concocting tasty dishes of seafood in cream sauce for the illustrious band of painters who lodged with her at various times—Diaz, Troyon, Daubigny, Corot, Jongkind and Courbet. It was at her table that Monet acquired the taste for good food that was to be his weakness in later life.

Although he took his meals with Mère Toutain he had a room at the Cheval Blanc, near the harbour. The view was superb and it was possible to paint in comfort even when the weather was bad. This snowscape, however, was a *plein air* painting, executed out of doors, as we know from an account given by a reporter on the *Journal du Havre* who surprised him at work. 'It was a bitterly cold day. We caught sight of a little stove, then an easel, and a man swathed in three greatcoats, with gloves on his hands, his face blue with cold: it was Monsieur Monet working on a snow effect.'

The above description tallies with Monet's passion for painting in all weathers, however severe. He continued to set up his easel outdoors throughout the terrible winter of 1879-80, and when he visited Norway habitually worked in temperatures of $-25°$.

THE WOMAN IN A GREEN DRESS, 1866

Monet painted this bravura picture in a mere four days in the spring of 1866. Despairing of finishing his large and ambitious canvas of *Le Déjeuner sur l'herbe* in time for the Salon, he feverishly set to work on a portrait of his young mistress Camille Doncieux. In the few months they had been together she had already posed several times for figures in *Le Déjeuner*. For this portrait he attired her in a sumptuous satin dress and a velvet jacket trimmed with fur, probably hired for the occasion—Monet wanted to make her look older, more sophisticated than the dewy nineteen-year-old she was in reality.

Recognizably in the genre of the society portrait, as produced by Alfred Stevens or Carolus Duran, the picture was accepted by the Salon jury, who forgave the detectable influence of Courbet, then execrated by the art establishment. The painting was well received by the public too, in spite of a few satirical jibes from certain of the critics, one of whom pretended not to know the difference between Monet and Manet. Manet was, understandably, less than delighted at the implied slight, and a meeting between the two painters was arranged by a mutual friend, Zacharie Astruc, to heal the breach. In the event the encounter was such a success that Manet became one of Monet's most loyal friends and supporters.

Zola, who at that time had not met Monet, wrote a highly favourable article for *L'Événement*: 'Here we have more than a realist, we have a subtle and powerful interpreter who has succeeded in rendering every detail without falling into the trap of sterility... Look at the dress. It is supple and substantial. It drapes softly, it is alive, and it proclaims the identity of the woman.'

Such acclaim made Monet believe that a brilliant career as a portrait painter awaited him, the more so as Arsène Housaye, editor of the review *L'Artiste* and a successful dramatist, had no hesitation in paying 800 francs to become the owner of *The Woman in a Green Dress*. For an unknown young painter it was a considerable sum of money. The collector intended the painting to pass on his death to the Musée du Luxembourg, the then equivalent of the Museum of Modern Art, but his son decided instead to put it up for auction.

Like all the young painters of his generation, Claude Monet longed to have a huge success at the Salon, the place where reputations were made. Anyone who won a medal or even a commendation was assured of fame and fortune. Hence this spectacular demonstration of his talents, which he hoped would win critical plaudits and bring commissions from private collectors and even from the state.

In May of the previous year Monet had installed himself at the inn in Chailly-en-Bière. There he had produced a number of studies for *Le Déjeuner sur l'herbe*, a tribute to Manet, whose manifesto-painting of that name had caused such a furore at the Salon des Refusés of 1863. With all the audacity of youth, Monet chose to execute these studies on six-metre lengths of canvas, a size previously attempted only by Courbet for his *Funeral at Ornans* and *The Studio*. Monet's plan was to show a group of contemporary figures in a leafy, sun-dappled landscape. His friends were enlisted as models, most notably Bazille, a fellow-student at the Atelier Gleyre, who sat for the male figures. It is not known if Courbet was also a model, but certainly one of the men bears a close resemblance to him; and it was Courbet, the great realist, who caused Monet to abandon his vast work. His advice made the younger painter realise the scale of the difficulties that faced him, and seeing that he had no hope of being ready for the Salon he simply gave up the whole project. Later the rolled-up canvas was given as security to the owner of the house in Argenteuil where Monet was living at the time; it was stored in a damp barn and was in a bad condition when the artist finally recovered possession of it in 1884. He was forced to cut away the rotten parts.

A year later, determined not to accept defeat, Monet embarked on another large canvas (although not quite on the same scale) showing human figures in an outdoor setting. This was *Women in the Garden*, which he started in the grounds of the house where he lived in Sèvres. The painting shows a group of elegant young women in pale summer dresses against a background of flowers and trees. The canvas was completed in Honfleur and submitted to the Salon of 1867, only to meet with a refusal. Although Émile Zola gave him moral support, the failure represented for Monet the start of a period of grave financial embarrassment, and he owed his very survival to Frédéric Bazille. Bazille came from a wealthy background, and he offered to purchase the painting for 2,500 francs, payable in monthly instalments of 50 francs. This arrangement continued until 1870, when the philanthropic young painter was killed in battle at Beaune-la-Rolande. Some years later, Bazille's father exchanged *Women in the Garden* for a portrait of his son by Renoir. The picture returned by a roundabout route to Monet and was finally bought by the state in 1921 for 200,000 francs.

Claude Monet

GARDEN WITH FLOWERS, 1866

While on a visit to his family in Le Havre during the summer of 1866, Monet painted two almost identical views of the garden at 'Le Coteau', the house at Sainte-Adresse which belonged to his aunt Lecadre. It was in this pleasant villa that the Monet and Lecadre families were in the habit of spending the summer.

Marie-Jeanne Lecadre was Adolphe Monet's widowed half-sister. Her husband, a prosperous wholesale grocer and ship's provisioner, had left her in comfortable circumstances and she took a keen interest in the progress of her two nephews, Claude and Léon, whose own mother had died while they were still children. An amateur painter herself and a lover of the arts, she was a close friend of the artist Armand Gautier, who encouraged Monet in his early years.

There were occasional disagreements between Claude and his aunt, who saw his future in terms of a conventional training at the École des Beaux-Arts. She was disappointed when he rejected academic painting and joined the small group of independents, but nevertheless continued to subsidize his studies until 1868.

This view of Le Coteau shows a typical Second Empire garden, with its bushes, broad borders of geraniums or selvias and standard roses with neat, round heads. The overall effect is pleasing, but gives no hint of the painter of light and transparency Monet was to become. It does however reflect an early love of gardens and flowers, the ruling passion of his later years.

The canvas became the property of the painter Antoine Guillemet (a friend of Manet who posed with Berthe Morisot for *The Balcony*). It was later purchased by Latouche, one of the few Parisian dealers who showed an interest in Claude Monet at the start of his career.

THE BEACH AT SAINTE-ADRESSE, 1867

In June 1867 Monet wrote to his friend Bazille, in Montpellier for the vacation: 'For the past fortnight I've been living in the bosom of the family, as well as is possible. Everyone is charming to me and admires every brushstroke I make.'

In the meantime Monet's young companion, Camille Doncieux, had remained behind in Paris. Living alone in a small room she was preparing for the birth of her baby, her sole support the medical student whom Monet had asked to take care of her while he went to make his peace with his father and aunt in Le Havre. They had been furious to learn of the girl's pregnancy and were threatening to cut off his allowance entirely.

Possibly it was to forget his troubles that Monet threw himself into work from the moment he arrived in Le Havre. First he painted the garden of his aunt's house in Sainte-Adresse, then his father and aunt sitting on the terrace watching the boats. The house fronted directly onto the beach and it was from this vantage point that Monet painted his scene of bathers watching the regatta. One of the spectators is Adolphe Monet. The fact that his father, and also his aunt and cousin, appear in so many of the pictures painted at this time would tend to suggest they had reconciled their differences. Not, however, to the extent of loosening the family purse strings, or not if one is to judge by Monet's desperate appeals to Bazille for help: Camille had no money, the child needed clothes, he himself could not afford the trip to Paris. Somehow he managed a few short visits, to be with his mistress and see his young son, but each time he was obliged to return dutifully to his family in Le Havre. It was spring 1868 before he was able to make the break and go back to Paris permanently, after an extremely productive period of work on the Normandy coast.

The Beach at Sainte-Adresse was not a controversial picture, and it was bought by a wealthy banker, one of the Hecht brothers: Henri Hecht was a devotee of Monet's work and owned several of his paintings, while his brother Albert was an avid collector of the works of Manet.

TERRACE AT SAINTE-ADRESSE, 1867

This canvas expresses all the euphoria of a fine summer's day. The red of the gladioli contrasts with the blue of the sea, specked with sailing boats, and in the distance are silhouetted the big steamers making for the harbour at Le Havre. Four people are relaxing on the terrace. In the foreground are Adolphe Monet and his half-sister, both seen from the back; they are sitting in garden chairs contemplating the scene stretching out before them. By the balustrade stands Claude's cousin Jeanne Lecadre, wearing a pale-coloured dress and chatting to a young man in a top hat. Peace and beauty reign supreme, reflecting the holiday mood prevailing in Sainte-Adresse.

The carefree atmosphere of this painting, which lay forgotten for years in the collection of an American cleric called Theodore Pitcairn, is in singular contrast to the facts of Monet's situation as we know them. Only a few weeks before, on 8 August 1867, Camille had given birth to a son, in circumstances of extreme poverty. Monet showed a remarkable ability to distance himself from his problems when he wrote to Bazille: 'Everything is fine here, work and family; were it not for the birth I should be the happiest man alive.'

Certainly the extended stay at Le Havre and Sainte-Adresse proved immensely productive as far as work was concerned. In the very first letter he wrote, in June, he spoke of twenty canvases under way, including the two Sainte-Adresse paintings. There was only one small cloud on the horizon: he had trouble with his eyes and was forced to stop work for a few days. In the event it proved no more than a trivial upset, but one remembers that in 1908 Monet's sight began to deteriorate, and in 1923 he was operated on to remove cataracts in both eyes.

MADAME GAUDIBERT, 1868

This is the only true society portrait ever painted by Monet. Looking at the elegant silhouette of the young woman in her satin dress, one is immediately reminded of the portraits of Alfred Stevens and Carolus Duran—in particular the latter's *Woman with a Glove* which, like Monet's *Madame Gaudibert*, was destined to end up in the Louvre.

Probably Monet was unenthusiastic about accepting the commission, but he was in desperate need of money—and the Gaudiberts were his principal supporters and patrons. Unlike most of their middle-class contemporaries, this family of wealthy Le Havre tradesmen were not in the least impressed by academic art, and even before taking an interest in Monet had collected works by Boudin and Armand Gautier, a realist painter who was a friend of Courbet. It was in fact Gautier, who had followed Monet's early career, who introduced him to Monsieur Gaudibert, in 1864. Over the years various members of the family bought paintings and commissioned portraits. The canvas of the young Madame Gaudibert was executed in the autumn of 1868, while the family were staying in their château of Ardennes Saint-Louis, near Le Havre. In terms of its composition the picture is entirely conventional, but Monsieur Gaudibert junior was well pleased, appreciating the beauty of the colouring and the fine painting of the dress and shawl. Monet was apparently paid only 130 francs, a low sum even for an early work, but it is possible he had already been given an advance, since he was always in need of money. The picture remained in the family until 1951, when it was acquired for the Louvre.

ICE FLOES ON THE SEINE, 1867

This little known canvas by Monet is something of a curiosity. The date is uncertain. It could have been painted in 1869-70, when Monet lived at Saint-Michel, near Bougival—the period when he worked with Renoir at the 'Grenouillère'. However, a more probable dating is 1867, favoured by Daniel Wildenstein, or even earlier, 1864-65. If Wildenstein is correct, the picture must have been executed during a brief visit to Bougival, at a time when Monet, short of money, was living with his family in Le Havre.

The particular interest of this snowscape is that it shows the clear influence of Japanese prints, and is fundamentally different from later works on a similar theme. Bracquemond possessed an extensive collection of Japanese prints, with which Monet was familiar. We know he studied them in some detail and absorbed many of their lessons in his own painting. Here one notices the extensive use of large areas of flat colour, reminiscent of Hiroshige and Hokusai, and the bold presentation, anticipating by some forty years the dramatic effects of foreshortening employed by the Nabis, and by Vuillard and Valotton in particular.

The canvas was left to the nation ten years ago by the collector Victor Lyon, a great admirer of the Impressionists.

THE MAGPIE, 1869

Once again Monet has returned to one of his favourite themes, the snowscape. The picture is dated winter 1868-69 and was painted near Étretat, where the artist was staying with his family. As ever, he was short of money and they were quibbling over his allowance. At least if he lived with them he was assured of food and shelter, although the unfortunate Camille was obliged to live in penury in Paris.

The painting has an anecdotal element that was perhaps directed towards the many collectors who loved nothing better than a painting that told a story. The Salon of the day was besieged with anecdotal pictures of the most appalling banality. *The Magpie* is of a different order of achievement altogether. The quality of the painting alone is exceptional. Monet needed an eye-catching feature to focus the scene; probably a magpie perched on the gate and supplied the solution.

In spite of this small nod in the direction of popular taste, the painting was rejected by the Salon jury of 1869, following a tirade from Gérôme, the most outspoken of the traditionalists, who railed against 'that group of madmen', as he described the young independents.

This time Monet simply could not allow himself to succumb to despair, matters were too serious for that as he now had a wife and child to support. With great courage he fought back, arranging an exhibition of his latest works at the gallery owned by Latouche, prominently situated on the corner of the rue Laffitte and the rue Lafayette. Latouche supported the avant-garde and had previously displayed *Women in the Garden* in his window. Monet also asked for help from his patron Monsieur Gaudibert, and thanks to his generosity was able to move to a peasant house in the small village of Saint-Michel, near Bougival. In the spring, with Renoir as his companion, he painted on the banks of the Seine. His scenes of the 'Grenouillère' and of young couples out on the river are among the most enchanting he ever painted.

THE TRAIN IN THE COUNTRYSIDE, 1870-71

This is Monet's first railway painting.   Utterly simply, it shows a train on the Paris-Saint-Germain line, with its typical two-tier coaches, running along a raised section of track.

It was Baudelaire who exhorted the young painters to depict scenes of modern life, and the group led by Manet, who met regularly at the Café Guerbois, devoted many a long evening to discussing the significance of modernity.   No doubt it was in response to one of these conversations that Monet painted this scene of a train in the countryside.   In the age of the machine, what could be more modern than the railways?   As early as 1844 Turner had painted his famous *Rain, Steam and Speed*, transforming the Great Western locomotive into a fantastic apparition emerging from swirling clouds of vapour.

This canvas by Monet dates from 1870, shortly before the painter left to spend the summer in Trouville.   Pissarro, van Gogh and Bonnard were not far behind him in experimenting with related motifs.   Monet himself returned to the theme on several later occasions, notably with his study of a train crossing an iron bridge over the Seine, painted in Argenteuil in 1874, and in a snowscape strongly reminiscent of Turner that shows a locomotive standing in the station at Argenteuil.   His culminating achievement is the series of views of the Gare Saint-Lazare, painted in 1877, a superbly personal treatment of the subject.

Readers of Proust will recognise in this view of the magnificent hotel and promenade at Trouville the atmosphere of the Hôtel de Balbec evoked in *À la recherche du temps perdu*—although in fact the fashionable society painted by Monet precedes that described by Proust by a full generation.   It is a luminous canvas, a glorious symphonic composition in which the sky, the flags flapping in the wind and the light dresses of the elegant summer visitors all play their part: a swan song of the Second Empire, age of the carefree and selfish pursuit of pleasure.   In many ways it seems curious that Monet was instantly drawn to a scene of such wordliness and frivolity, since it corresponded to nothing in his own character.   But he had no hesitation in turning his back on the harbour and the boats and installing himself on the pier, whence he could command a view of a vast panorama that took in the throng of bathers and the sunlit façade of the hotel.   The sea is the *raison d'être* of the composition, and yet its presence is no more than hinted at.   In this above all the picture differs from the scenes of fashionable life painted by Boudin a few years before, where the sea itself is always the central feature.

Of course, it is likely that it was not so much the modish character of the scene that fascinated Monet, but rather the interplay of the pale colours of the dresses, the illuminated façades and the effect of passing clusters of cloud against the broad sweep of the sky.

On 19 July came news of the outbreak of the Franco-Prussian War, but Monet was bound up in his work and did not appreciate the gravity of the situation.   It was not until the French surrendered and Gambetta set about raising an army of 500,000 that he began to be seriously concerned.   Even so, he did not expect to be personally affected by the order to mobilize as his family had paid for a substitute as long ago as 1863, at the time of his military service, and he assumed that another young man would go to be killed in his place.   He went to Le Havre seeking news and found himself caught up in the panic that had swept through the town.   Amid the general confusion he fled to England, leaving Camille behind with their baby in Trouville.   It was his loyal friend Boudin who looked after the family and arranged for their safe passage across the Channel.

CAMILLE ON THE BEACH, 1870

Camille Doncieux was seven years younger than Monet. The couple met in 1865, shortly after Monet returned from Algeria. She posed for him while he was working on *Le Déjeuner sur l'herbe*, and was the model for the virtuoso piece *The Woman in a Green Dress*, which was such a success at the Salon of 1866 that Monet flirted with the idea of making society portraiture his career. Right up to her death she sat for him regularly, appearing frequently as a female figure in a rural landscape. Some of these canvases are among Monet's masterpieces.

Shortly before leaving Paris for Trouville, Camille and Claude were married in a civil ceremony performed at the town hall of the eighth arrondissement. Courbet was one of the witnesses. Camille's parents were present, and the affair was conducted with proper formality. All that marred the occasion was the absence of Monet's father and aunt, who regarded the union as a disastrous misalliance. The Doncieux family had the foresight to insist on a marriage settlement that allowed their daughter to retain control of her own small dowry, an insurance against the prodigal instincts of their future son-in-law.

While they were staying in Trouville, Monet painted many scenes of Camille on the beach, in various poses. Although the pictures resemble one another closely, it is possible that she was not the only model Monet used. This particular portrait, however, is almost certainly of Camille; Monet never sold it and it remained in the possession of their second son, Michel, until he died.

CAMILLE READING, 1871

This tender portrait is a rarity in Monet's *œuvre*, resembling more the genre of portrait favoured by Manet, Degas or James Tissot. It shows the young Camille in contemplative mood, and the setting is an interior of the family's London home. Although Monet had arrived in England almost penniless, with assistance from the dealer Durand-Ruel he was able to rent a comfortably furnished flat in Kensington. Their stay in London was on the whole a happy one, except for the news from France, which told of the defeat of the French army, the death of Bazille, and the establishment of the Commune.

With his financial problems taken care of, Monet was able to devote himself wholeheartedly to painting. This portrait of Camille reading was one of the first products of his eight months in London. There are also views of the Thames, of Green Park and Hyde Park, the Port of London and the Houses of Parliament. Such was the affection Monet developed for the look of the city that he returned there on at least seven occasions between 1870 and 1901, in all producing more than one hundred canvases of the English capital.

This charming portrait was submitted by Durand-Ruel to the International Exhibition in South Kensington; he bought it subsequently for 500 francs, although not until two years later. The canvas was then acquired by a close friend of Marcel Proust, the Princesse de Montbéliard (later the Princesse de Polignac) who in turn sold it at auction in 1899. The canvas was bought by the collector Raymond Koechlin for 5,700 francs, and he left it to the Louvre in 1931, together with a number of other Impressionist masterpieces.

After the suppression of the Commune, Monet was free to leave London, but he took his time about returning to Paris. Together with his wife and child he spent five months, from June to November 1871, in the small port of Zaandam, twelve kilometres from Amsterdam.

Why he chose Zaandam, or indeed visited Holland at all, we have no idea. Possibly it was because he had heard of it from Daubigny, who had worked there a few years earlier. At all events he was enchanted by the look of Holland, the marvellous cloud formations in the broad sky, the picturesque windmills in the polders and the ornately decorated houses fronting the canals. 'There's a lifetime's painting here,' he wrote soon after his arrival to Pissarro, who had remained in London. His words echo Rembrandt's declaration that you could spend all your life painting without moving from the spot.

Thanks to the payments from Durand-Ruel and the money earned by Camille, who gave French lessons to the children of the prosperous burghers of Zaandam, Monet was able to work in peace. Enthused by these new visual stimuli he painted like one possessed, devoting no more than a few hours to the great museums of Amsterdam. His signature appears in the visitors' book at the Rijksmuseum, where he particularly admired the Vermeers. He painted in all twenty-four canvases while he was in Holland, among them this tranquil view of the town hall and the quayside by the Zaan.

The Dutch landscapes were much admired when they were exhibited by Durand-Ruel. This particular canvas was bought by Étienne Moreau-Nélaton in 1872. Others were purchased by Daubigny, the baritone J.-B. Faure, Charles Deudon, who owned the Old England shops, Ernest Hoschedé and the banker Ernest May, one of Monet's most loyal collectors.

THREE FIGURES UNDER THE LILACS, 1872

The title of this picture is disputed—it is also known as *Lilacs, grey weather*—but it was certainly painted in the spring of Claude Monet's first year in Argenteuil.

Having spent more than a year away, in England and Holland, Monet wanted to live near the Seine, within easy reach of his favourite painting spots. It was on Manet's recommendation, and with financial assistance from him, that he settled in Argenteuil at the end of 1871. His time there was to be one of the happiest and most productive periods of his life. The money from sales to Durand-Ruel and various other collectors permitted the couple to live in comfort. Monet entertained on a grand scale, Camille posed for him in ravishing ensembles, and the household now extended to two servants and a nursemaid for young Jean.

Monet was enchanted by his new surroundings and never tired of setting up his easel on the banks of the Seine, painting boats, oarsmen and yachts. He also turned his attention to the nearby fields of poppies and painted the metal railway bridge that spanned the Seine—a concession to modernism. The times were euphoric and the mood of happiness infected Monet's other painter friends: Renoir, Pissarro and Sisley all came and worked at Argenteuil. Even Manet, hitherto no lover of open-air painting, often worked at Monet's side—sometimes including him in his pictures. These are the canvases in which Manet came closest to the spirit of Impressionism, although that word was not then used to describe the independent artists whose standard-bearer he had, however unintentionally, become.

It is not clear if Camille was one of the models for this exquisite and subtle canvas, but the man lying at the woman's feet is certainly Sisley, who was visiting Monet at Argenteuil. The quality of the painting so impressed the connoisseur Étienne Moreau-Nélaton that he bought it in order to present it to the Louvre.

This exquisite picture, of subtle and delicate colouring, was included in the second exhibition of the Impressionist group, held in 1876. It was bought by Caillebotte, who bequeathed it to the state, so that Monet had the satisfaction of seeing one of his works accepted by the museums commission.

The canvas anticipates by thirty years the 'domestic' scenes of Bonnard. It is not so much the representation of a lovely scene, more a hymn of praise to pleasure itself, enshrining everything Monet held most dear—his wife, a tall white silhouette passing in the background, his young son Jean, who is seated on the ground, the charming blossom-filled garden and, above all, the artfully arranged table with its bowls of fruit, silver coffee-pot and coffee cups. Monet was something of a sybarite and relished good food, fine wines and spirits. He never forgot the wonderful specialities concocted by the Mère Toutain at the Ferme Saint-Siméon, near Honfleur. In this he was a typical product of his background—in the French bourgeois homes of the day food was always plentiful and of the highest quality.

After 1883, when success and fortune were assured, Monet was able to indulge his gourmandise to the full. René Gimpel, who stayed at Giverny in 1918, recalled, on the one hand, the splendid *Waterlilies* presented to him by Monet, and on the other hand the wonderful meal the chef had prepared: *hors-d'œuvre* made with the 'best Normandy butter', sweetbreads with spinach, roast chicken—which everyone declined—chicken with black olives, a delicious tart and fruit 'as beautiful to look at as flowers'.

Right up to his last years Monet remained a formidable trencherman, accompanying his lavish meals with Normandy wines and finishing with 'a little glass of something stronger'. 'Not such a little glass either,' as Gimpel tells us.

This jewel of Impressionist painting conveys to perfection the sensation of the warm wind and the scented grass, the serenity and glowing light of a fine summer's day.

Monet was obviously pleased with the picture as he showed it at the first Impressionist exhibition, held at Nadar's studio in 1874. It has all the hallmarks of Impressionism: it was painted out of doors, it shows a scene of everyday life—Camille and Jean running down a grassy slope—the colours are light and it is strongly atmospheric.

The painter's opinion of his work was apparently shared by the two collectors who, in turn, owned the painting: J.-B. Faure and Étienne Moreau-Nélaton. The former was a famous baritone who sang in Gounod's *Faust* at the Opéra; he had a positive mania for collecting and owned 67 works by Manet and almost as many Monets. The latter was himself a talented painter and a fine judge of pictures. The Impressionist paintings he acquired, together with the Caillebotte collection, today form the basis of the superb display in the Jeu de Paume Gallery.

Monet's Argenteuil period is often identified with his paintings of the Seine. But in the course of those seven years he also produced numerous snow scenes, gardens, apple trees in blossom, views of the village, portraits of Camille and Jean and still lifes—not to mention the landscapes executed during visits to Rouen, Le Havre, Étretat and Paris, and also briefly to Holland. On his second Dutch trip he concentrated largely on Amsterdam, which he had barely seen on his way back from London in 1871.

One can only marvel at the creative drive that produced 237 paintings in 7 years, a veritable golden age of painting.

IMPRESSION: SUNRISE, 1873

As famous as the *Mona Lisa* or *The Night Watchman*, this canvas was executed in the spring of 1873, while Monet was staying in Le Havre. It was probably completed in a single session, at dawn.

Although not essentially different in spirit from the other Monets shown at the first Impressionist exhibition, held in 1874 at Nadar's rooms on the Boulevard des Capucines, it was singled out for censure and abuse by critics and public alike. This may have been partly because its title was seen as provocative, though it was not in fact new and had previously been used by Huet and Chintreuil. Louis Leroy, the critic for *Charivari* (not the most high-minded of periodicals,) claimed to find its name irresistibly funny and made it the particular butt of his article. He introduced the figure of an old academic painter, a pupil of David, who came to see the exhibition. After studying the works of Pissarro, Degas and Sisley, the old man paused before Monet's canvas.

'What does this canvas represent?' he asked. 'Look at the label.'

'Impression: Sunrise.'

'Impression, I thought as much. I was impressed, and I thought to myself, yes, there's bound to be an impression in there somewhere… and what freedom, what ease in the handling! Designs for wallpaper are more finished than this seascape!'

By the end of his tour, old Vincent had become quite mad and started doing a scalp dance, shouting: 'Wah Wah Wah!… I am the impression that advances, the avenging palette knife!'

Impressionism had found its name. Although taken aback at first, the artists adopted with pride the description that had been intended as an insult. In spite of all the ridicule it attracted *Impression: Sunrise* immediately found a buyer. It was purchased by Ernest Hoschedé for 800 francs, a not inconsiderable sum for a work that was regarded as little more than a sketch. It was re-sold at a loss some years later, for 210 francs, to Dr de Bellio, a Rumanian collector who often came to Monet's aid in his darkest days. Together with other Monets, the painting was bequeathed to the Musée Marmottan by the collector's daughter.

Beyond price as a historical document and as a painting in its own right, it was stolen in 1985.

SUMMER, THE MEADOW, 1874

This painting shows Monet at his most relaxed. It is a charming interlude, full of tenderness and grace. He painted it *en plein air* in the plain to the west of Argenteuil, away from the ripples and reflections of the river he loved. His subject is once again Camille, this time sitting on the grass reading. She wears a feathered hat; a respectable woman of the day could not be seen without some form of head-covering, even on a country walk.

The canvas belongs in spirit with *Wild Poppies*, and is redolent of peace and happiness. It recalls the serenity of the Trouville portraits, but here the handling is altogether lighter and more fluid. Durand-Ruel and other collectors sometimes urged Monet to make his canvases look more finished, but he was interested only in a spontaneous rendering of the moment. This scene is painted, as it were, with the tip of the brush, the sky limpid, the trees barely sketched in—reminiscent of Corot—the young woman suggested rather than expressed as an individual human form. It is a typical example of Impressionism at its peak. One recalls Cézanne's dictum: 'Monet is just an eye, but what an eye. He's the best of us all.'

Shown at the second exhibition of the Impressionist group, the painting was put up for auction at the Hôtel Drouot in March 1875 but failed to find a buyer. Money problems again threatened to plunge Monet into the nightmare of debt which he hoped he had put behind him for ever.

SAILING BOATS AT ARGENTEUIL, 1875

The exact date of this work has never been established. Monet painted boats and yachts throughout his seven years in Argenteuil, and some believe the work dates from as early as 1872. Here the boats are preparing to set off from the landing stage on the Petit-Genevilliers bank. It is possible that the yachtsmen are Gustave Caillebotte and his friends, since it is his house that can be seen behind the trees. The wealthy engineer loved sailing and built his own racing boats. He had links with the Impressionist group through Degas, who was impressed enough with his painting to offer advice and encouragement. Living in the little village of Petit-Genevilliers, right opposite Argenteuil, it was inevitable that he should associate with Claude Monet, and during the black years of the seventies he took over the role of Maecenas assumed in a previous decade by Frédéric Bazille. There are innumerable letters from Monet begging for his help.

With uncharacteristic loyalty Monet sprang to Caillebotte's defence when Pissarro and Gauguin wanted him removed from the group. Announcing firmly that Caillebotte was his friend, he succeeded in imposing his will on the rest. Although Caillebotte's *œuvre* amounts to some 300 pictures and is by no means negligible, his principal contribution to Impressionism lay in the bequest of his collection to the state in 1894. The Museums Commission in charge of acquisitions were caught in a classic conflict of interest. They did not dare turn Caillebotte down flat, but on the other hand they feared the reaction of the academic painters if they accepted his gift. Their compromise was to accept half of the legacy—38 paintings out of 67. Monet fared better than most as 8 out of 16 of his works were taken, among them *Sailing Boats at Argenteuil.* Today they are among the glories of the Jeu de Paume Gallery.

This brilliant canvas, its gleaming red boats casting their shadows onto blue water, was painted near the bridge at Argenteuil where the local yachtsmen were in the habit of overhauling their boats.   It is possible that Monet painted it from his 'floating studio', enabling him to take in the two banks of the Seine at once.

Monet had dreamed of possessing his own boat-cum-studio ever since he saw Daubigny's 'Bottin', which the landscapist used to move easily from one site to another along the River Oise.   Soon after moving to Argenteuil, Monet bought a flat-bottomed wherry and had a carpenter construct a tall cabin where he could paint sheltered from the sun, rain and cold.   A separate area at the back was covered with a striped awning.   Monet was very fond of his boat and painted it on several occasions, as too did Manet when he came to visit.   Later, when Monet moved to Vétheuil and then to Poissy, he took it with him.   It is likely that it survived even into the Giverny era.

This canvas is one of the most finished of all the series of sailing boats.   It was started from life but undoubtedly completed in the studio, judging by the care taken over the details of the craft.   There is no indication that Monet ever exhibited the picture, and no record of it at all until 1921, when it was purchased by the American painter Romaine Brooks.   She was a portraitist who painted society people and fashionable writers in a palette restricted to greys, whites and blacks; among her works are portraits of Jean Cocteau and Gabriele d'Annunzio, with whom she had a tempestuous affair.   *Argenteuil* was subsequently sold at auction to Madame Jean Walter, who left it to the state, together with the rest of her magnificent collection.   By this route one of the masterpieces of Monet's Argenteuil period found its way to the Orangerie, where it is exhibited in conjunction with the major *Waterlilies* sequence.

The full title of the painting is *The Promenade, Woman with a Parasol.* Its grace and elegance and euphoric mood make it one of the most characteristic Impressionist works; and it is without doubt one of the most appealing female portraits in Monet's entire *œuvre*, undeniably a labour of love.

The female in question is of course the delightful Camille, on this occasion accompanied by her young son Jean, now a sturdy boy. Whereas in other portraits of his wife Monet barely particularized her features, in this inspired picture he has tried to capture her fresh beauty and casual elegance. Even in his later portraits of the Hoschedé daughters he did not surpass this striking tableau of youthful beauty.

The impassioned, whiplash brushwork is quite remarkable: the figure stands out vivaciously against the cloudy sky. Curiously, Monet seems to have devoted a lot more time to filling in the detail of the grass at Camille's feet. Presumably he finished that section in the studio, leaving untouched the figure he had completed from the motif.

These were, sadly, the last of the fine days for Camille. She was soon to become pregnant for the second time, and was then taken gravely ill after giving birth to a second son, Michel. Perhaps it was an artist's premonition that made Monet paint her over and over again, as though he wanted to create many images of her before the original disappeared for ever.

After forming part of various private collections, the portrait of Camille was bought at auction in 1965 by the American collector Paul Mellon. The French authorities made no move to prevent the picture leaving the country.

TRAIN IN THE SNOW, 1875

Less influenced than Manet or Degas by Baudelaire's and the Goncourt brothers' insistence that modern life was the primary subject of art, Monet did nevertheless turn on several occasions to themes of which they would have heartily approved. The two great works of his youth, *Le Déjeuner sur l'herbe* and *Women in the Garden*, are perhaps the most obvious examples. But there are others, such as *The Luncheon* and *The Dinner* of 1868, and the delightful views of La Grenouillère and the beach at Trouville. It is not therefore particularly surprising that Monet should have shown an interest in the railways, a modern theme *par excellence.* Living near the station at Argenteuil, he had ample opportunity to observe the trains as they embarked and disembarked their freight of passengers.

What appealed to him most about this scene was the effect of the snow and the smoke from the locomotive, which is shown as a sort of black monster with glowing eyes.

The collector Dr de Bellio was immediately attracted by the subject and bought the painting direct from Monet, bypassing Durand-Ruel.

MADAME MONET WITH HER SON, 1875

This delightfully affectionate portrait is in fact misnamed. It certainly represents Camille, but the child playing at her feet could not be Jean—by 1875 he was an eight-year-old boy. And Michel Monet was not born until 1878.

The painting is remarkable in several respects. It is one of Monet's finest portraits of his wife, approaching Renoir in style. For the first time Monet has used the device of massed flowers placed horizontally along the top of the picture, a scheme he used often in his Giverny period when painting the garden in front of his house. Also noteworthy is the spirited and expressive treatment of the pleated dress.

One sad detail. This charming canvas is the last detailed likeness of Camille; in general Monet preferred not to particularize his portraits. Here it is evident that he deliberately chose to do so.

LE PARC MONCEAU, 1876

Claude Monet always kept a *pied-à-terre* in Paris; first at the rue d'Isly, later at rue Moncey, rue d'Edimbourg and rue de Vintimille. These various apartments he used to store pictures and for business meetings with clients and dealers. For many years, while he was hard up, the rents were paid by Manet or Caillebotte.

All these addresses were near the Parc Monceau and Monet naturally turned to the vistas, both natural and artificial, offered by this recent creation of Napoleon III. It was a popular and fashionable spot. Monet could not bear to let a single day pass without working, and although the park could not compare in beauty with Argenteuil, since he was forced to visit Paris from time to time he put his leisure hours to profitable use. There are two other almost identical canvases of this motif.

There may have been another reason why Monet was drawn to the Parc Monceau. Like many other elegant Parisiennes, Madame Hoschedé was in the habit of taking her children for walks there every day, and we know that the wife of one of his most loyal collectors had begun to assume a special significance in his life.

Early in 1877 Monet embarked on what was to become a series of paintings of the Gare Saint-Lazare, although initially he planned only a single canvas. He had long been attracted by the constantly changing effects observable in the station: the sunlight intensified by the glass panes, the play of steam and smoke. This station was a familiar sight since early childhood, being the terminus for Le Havre and the Normandy coast. When he lived in Argenteuil it was again on his route.

In 1873 Manet had painted the view from the Pont de l'Europe, and Caillebotte had used a similar theme four years later. But in both these cases the setting was little more than a background for the human characters: in Manet's *The Railway* a girl with her governess, and in Caillebotte's *Pont de l'Europe* a group of men in frock-coats and top hats. And in the latter painting the real protagonist might be said to be the architecture of the bridge itself.

Monet was interested uniquely in the effects of light, sunshine, steam and smoke. He was barely concerned with the figures, which he indicated by a sort of shorthand. Another difference: Manet and Caillebotte looked down over the station, Monet put himself on a level with the platforms. In practice, no easy matter. To work from the motif he was obliged to take up position during the busiest times of day. All the canvases were in fact completed in the studio, a practice of which he did not really approve. 'My studio is in the open air,' he used to say. It was however a measure he had to resort to quite often, in particular for his more finished pieces. And this station series is painted with the greatest possible care and attention to detail.

In a sense 'series' is a misnomer, since no one painting is shown from the same angle as another; in that respect the sequence differs from the *Haystacks* and *Rouen Cathedral.*

Shown at the third exhibition of the Impressionist group, the canvas was an immediate success, in particular with Zola, who wrote: 'That is where painting has arrived at today... our artists should discover the poetry of stations, just as their fathers before them discovered the poetry of forests and rivers.' Later, when he wrote *La Bête humaine*, Zola must have remembered this Monet painting, for his description of the station tallies exactly with the painter's vision.

Monet's most assiduous collectors all shared the author's enthusiasm; the twelve canvases were borne off by Ernest Hoschedé, Dr de Bellio and Caillebotte for sums of between 400 and 700 francs each.

This picture could almost have been painted by one of the Fauves, Vlaminck or Derain.   It does not, as once thought, commemorate the first 14 July celebrations, but the International Exhibition of 30 June 1878, symbol of the renaissance of France after the defeat of 1870.   Monet was staying in Paris at the time and was struck by the mood of rejoicing in the flag-hung streets.   His colleague Manet chose to stay in the elegant seventeenth arrondissement, where he painted *Rue Mosnier Decked Out with Flags*, but Monet went to the working-class area of Les Halles, and stationed himself on a balcony which afforded a prospect of the rue Montorgueil aflutter with tricolours.   As he told René Gimpel, he had simply asked the tenant's permission to set up his easel.   It is highly probable that he painted the companion picture *Rue Saint-Denis Decked Out with Flags* on the same day.   The two pictures are similar in style, with rapid, energetic brushwork.

This picture passed through many hands and was much in demand by collectors.   Shown for the first time at the fourth Impressionist exhibition, in 1879, it was bought initially by Dr de Bellio and then passed to the collection of the Prince de Wagram, a young officer descended from Maréchal Berthier, whose taste for avant-garde art appalled his family.   When he was killed in the last days of the 1914-18 War, his heirs lost no time in selling off the paintings, and today these form the nucleus of one of the great French collections.   This particular painting was bought by the playwright Alfred Savoir.

Its companion piece enjoyed equal success.   It was snapped up by Ernest Hoschedé against considerable competition, and later came into the hands of the composer Emmanuel Chabrier, who had the happy notion of using the inheritance left by his wife to build up a collection of modern painting.   In this way the man best known for writing *Espana* became the proud owner of Manet's *The Bar at the Folies-Bergère*, three Renoirs, six Monets, two Sisleys and a Cézanne!

Monet painted this sequel to the earlier *Parc Monceau* at a time when he had been forced to make a hasty departure from Argenteuil, where he was being pursued by creditors.   Together with Camille and Jean he took refuge at 26 rue d'Edimbourg, his *pied-à-terre* in Paris.   Here his wife gave birth to their second son, Michel.   Lack of money meant that conditions were far from ideal and Camille's health never recovered.   She became steadily more ill over the following months and died a year later.

This canvas is in complete contrast to the *Rue Montorgueil Decked Out with Flags*, although it was painted at about the same time.   It is hard to believe that the artist who painted this sober tree-filled landscape also conjured up that vivid scene of celebration.   But, as was once said of Ingres, Monet had 'many brushes'.

This is certainly one of Monet's last Parisian paintings, possibly the last of all.   A few months later he moved with his family to Vétheuil and thereafter returned to Paris only for the briefest of visits.

The true 'subject matter' of the picture is the play of sunlight on the leaves, a theme that had obsessed Monet since he was a young man and painted *Le Déjeuner sur l'herbe* and *Women in the Garden.*

On the night of 5-6 January 1880, the village of Vetheuil awoke to the sound of loud explosions and crackings. The Seine, which had been frozen over since 10 December, was literally splitting apart, the ice was breaking up. Monet went out to watch and to rescue his boats. At dawn he began to paint the devastated landscape. Three days later he wrote to Dr de Bellio: 'The break-up of the ice has been terrible and naturally I tried to do something with it, which I will show you on my next visit.'

Monet was fascinated by the apocalyptic vision of the ice-floes drifting along the Seine under lowering skies. He needed to work quickly before the thaw set in, so there was no time to seek out picturesque angles or vantage points, he simply painted what he could see from the bank near his house. The canvases are composed for the most part of vertical and horizontal strokes, the former representing the trees beside the river, and the latter the drifting ice-floes: the pictures show a large measure of uniformity, presaging the direction he was to take in his later series.

In his monograph on Claude Monet and his works, published forty years later, Gustave Geffroy wrote of these paintings: 'Under the pale sky, sinister and at the same time beautiful, the familiar landscape is strewn with broken ice, the greeny waters are still frozen to their depths. The cruel poem of winter is written in these canvases, in which Monet has captured the frozen apparitions of the air and water, the cold, vibrant reverberations (*sic*) beneath the solidified surface of the river, the stupor of the vegetation trapped in the northern light, ghostly trees hung with frost, funereal poplars, ravaged hillsides, between the dull sky and the water shot with metallic light.'

Claude and Camille Monet had moved to Vétheuil, together with Ernest Hoschedé's family, in 1878. Life for the joint household was impossibly hard in that winter of 1879-80. At Christmas the temperature was 25 degrees below zero and Alice Hoschedé, in charge of the domestic arrangements, had no money for coal or wood. Monet was sunk in depression: Camille was dead and he had the responsibility of two small children; there were few collectors interested in buying his work and money was shorter than ever. Happily this state of affairs was not to endure. A landscape of Lavacourt was accepted shortly afterwards for the Salon, inspiring the faithful Zola to write: 'In ten years time he (Monet) will be a success, his works will be hung and he will receive his due reward. He will sell his pictures for huge sums of money and stand at the head of the modern movement.'

There was cause for optimism when Durand-Ruel again started buying Monet's pictures. The memory of bad times began to fade.

ILE SAINT-MARTIN, VETHEUIL, 1880

The full title of this charming picture is *Path through the Poppies, Ile Saint-Martin.* It dates from Monet's Vétheuil period, one of the bleakest times of his life. Little money was coming in, the winter had been appallingly harsh, and Camille had died only the previous year. In 1878 the Hoschedé family had moved with Monet and his dependents to Vétheuil, near Mantes, and Monet now lived there with Alice Hoschedé and her six children. Still youthful and elegant, although she was not to keep her good looks and svelte figure for long, she became the companion of the second half of Monet's life. In 1880 she had not yet severed her ties with Ernest Hoschedé, who remained in Paris to try to rescue something from his disastrous bankruptcy. Officially Alice was there only to help Monet with the care of his two small sons while he was recovering from Camille's death. In his latter years Monet proudly insisted that he had never once given his children an order. One must assume he was exaggerating: both boys could read and write, and Michel Monet was sent to England to learn English.

In spite of the profound misery of his bereavement, Monet worked unremittingly while he was at Vétheuil. In the winter of 1879-80 he painted the break-up of the ice on the Seine and numerous other snowscapes; these are characterized by a rapidity of handling reminiscent of *Impression: Sunrise* and are full of atmosphere and feeling. In the spring he painted rural landscapes, wonderful apple trees in blossom and scenes on the banks of the Seine, distinguished by a marvellous sense of colouring.

Monet needed to work hard to support the extended family for which he now assumed responsibility. Happily Durand-Ruel had emerged from the financial crisis that overwhelmed him early in 1874, and was now ready to start buying pictures again. Although Monet complained constantly of being penniless, there were in fact more and more collectors eager to own his paintings. A recent addition to their number was Charles Ephrusi, a banker who was also the proprieter of the influential *Gazette des Beaux-Arts*, and Proust's model for the character of Swann. He bought this view of the Ile Saint-Martin for 400 francs only a few days after it was finished. A great connoisseur and a friend of Renoir—he appears as a man in a top-hat in one of his riverside paintings—Charles Ephrusi proved a faithful friend to Monet. He also persuaded his sister Beatrix de Rothschild to buy some of Monet's works.

GIRL SEATED BENEATH A WILLOW, 1880

Alice Hoschedé is the model for the woman sitting in the grass reading.   It is one of the rare paintings of her by Monet, who probably wanted to avoid unduly provoking her husband.   Although Ernest seemed no longer very attached to his wife, he was an occasional visitor to Vétheuil, and if he was expected Monet would simply absent himself and go on a painting trip to the Normandy coast.   It was not until after the death of Hoschedé—who by then had become a respected art critic—that the couple were able, with relief, to cease the pretence.   On 10 July 1892 they were married.   By then Alice was a stout matron with a sharp tongue and a commanding air; Monet no longer painted her, preferring to use her daughters as sitters.

This delightful scene bears a strong resemblance to *Summer, the Meadow*, painted six years before, which shows Camille in a similar attitude.

This riot of sunflowers is Monet's brilliant gesture of farewell to the poverty and grief that marked his time in Vétheuil. In the autumn of 1881 he was making preparations to move nearer to Paris, to Poissy, where Zola had helped him find a house.

The two children who can be seen on the path are the two youngsters of the household, Michel Monet and Jean-Pierre Hoschedé, separated in age by no more than a few months. The latter was Monet's favourite and he painted him on several occasions, lending support to the notion that he was the child's father. Jean-Pierre Hoschedé always denied this, but in middle age and towards the end of his life he carefully cultivated an evident resemblance. He wrote a book of memoirs which is the best account we have of Monet's domestic life.

At the time he left Vétheuil, Monet was still experiencing financial difficulties, and owed six payments in rent to his landlord. He was ordered to pack up and leave within twenty-four hours, but in the event was granted a reprieve. This was to be Monet's last such undignified departure. In February 1881 Durand-Ruel had again started dealing in Monet's paintings and, although he had temporary problems of liquidity, he never again abandoned Monet. The painter was free to plan ahead and embark on new and ambitious projects.

Monet's time in Poissy was punctuated by numerous trips to the Normandy coast. The canvases he returned with were hugely successful and he was regarded as the undisputed leader of the Impressionist group.

There are four versions of the *Garden in Vétheuil*, all of which were bought by American collectors.

THE DOUANIER'S COTTAGE, 1882

Monet did several paintings of this hut on the cliffs near Pourville—called variously *The Fisherman's Hut* or *The Douanier's Cottage* or *Cabin.* Cottages like this were built all along the coast under Napoleon I, at the time of the continental blockade; they were occupied by coastguards or customs officers. After the fall of the Empire the buildings were taken over by fishermen, who used them to repair their nets.

The 'cottage' series marks Monet's return to the Normandy coast. His first port of call was Dieppe, and he then moved on to an inn in the little village of Pourville, only a few kilometres away from the fashionable resort. To Monet's delight the landlord of the inn, Paul Graff (known as Père Paul), proved to be a superb cook with a vast repertoire of Normandy and Alsace specialities. Such was Monet's pleasure that he made a present to the Graff family of the portraits he did of them—an unprecedented gesture from one who had a reputation for being tight-fisted.

THE BEACH AND CLIFFS AT ETRETAT, 1883

Monet did not like Poissy and left in midwinter to work in Étretat. The weather was so bad that he was forced to return home after two or three weeks, but he went back there in three successive years. He was particularly fascinated by the dramatic cliff formations and the vista of fishing boats hauled up on the beach. Étretat was a subject he never tired of—indeed he produced so many canvases on the theme that Gauguin described it as 'steam-powered production'.

On a trip to Étretat two years later, Monet met Guy de Maupassant, who owned a villa there called La Guillette. Curiously, these two very different men got on famously and spent many evenings together in the local cafés, chatting over a carafe of calvados. Monet wrote to Alice Hoschedé that he doubted, even so, whether Maupassant really understood his work. However, in 1886, the novelist wrote a long article in *Gil Blas* that demonstrated a quite remarkable insight into Monet's methods and intentions: 'I have often followed Claude Monet in his search for impressions. He would cease really to be a painter and become a hunter instead. Coming face to face with his subject (the painter) paused, watching for the sun and the shadows, and with a few brushstrokes plucked a ray of sun as it fell, or a passing flurry of snow, and scorning the false or conventional set them down rapidly on the canvas. I have seen him capturing in this way a sparkling flood of light over the white cliff, fixing it in a spray of yellow tones that conveyed the effect of this intangible, blinding brilliance in a strange and quite unexpected way. Another time he seized in both hands a downpour of rain over the sea and literally threw it onto the canvas.'

In 1883, when this canvas was painted, Monet was in a state of depression, worried that he would not be ready for the exhibition of his work Durand-Ruel was holding on March 1. Bad weather was holding him up and he would be obliged to finish the series in the studio.

The exhibition went ahead as planned, but the painter's pessimism was justified to the extent that it was only a partial success. Several canvases were nonetheless sold, among them this one, which was bought by a businessman from Bayonne called Antonin Personnaz. A lover of Impressionism, he assembled a fine collection which passed on his death to the Louvre.

Claude Monet was at the absolute peak of his powers when he painted this vigorous, almost violent canvas, with brushstrokes of whiplash intensity. He was forty-six years old and had recently painted one of his rare self-portraits: a man with a stubborn brow, topped by a Basque beret, eyebrows drawn together in a frown, with the penetrating gaze and determined air of a man who knows what he wants. The canvases executed at Belle-Ile are among the most forceful and incisive of his entire *œuvre*.

He arrived at the Belle-Ile on 15 September and made his headquarters in a village on the stormy Atlantic coast, directly overlooking the sea. Together with an old fisherman called Poly, who carried his materials, he would go out in all weathers to paint from the motif, donning an oilskin to work at the height of a storm, his easel lashed by flying stones. Once he was nearly swept away by the waves, but he rejoiced in the spectacle of the ocean churning and surging, flinging itself against the unyielding rocks.

Unlike the canvases of the Normandy coast, these employ very strong tones, reds and bright blues. They look ahead to the world of the Fauves, which was not to come into being until twenty years later. Monet was aware that this group of paintings was very different. 'I don't know if the work I bring back will be to everyone's taste,' he wrote to Durand-Ruel, 'but what I do know is that this coast enthrals me.'

Monet had lodgings in a fisherman's house but took his meals at the village inn, where he sated himself on shellfish and crabs to the point that even he finally tired of the diet, and was heartily glad to receive an invitation to visit the painter John Russell, who lived in a nearby village.

It was at the inn one October evening that Monet met the critic Gustave Geffroy, who was on holiday in the area. The reviewer for *La Justice* had frequently written about Monet's work but the two men had never met. Geffroy, who was to be president of the Académie Goncourt, became Monet's literary patron, writing numerous articles and prefaces devoted to him, and also a book, published in 1922, which unfortunately is full of factual errors. Through Geffroy, Monet was to rediscover Georges Clemenceau, whom he had not seen for twenty years. Clemenceau became his closest friend and support in his old age.

When Monet left Belle-Ile on 25 November, the weather having taken a turn for the worse, he returned to Giverny with a veritable feast of paintings, thirty-nine splendid canvases that form the solid kernel of an *œuvre* hitherto devoted to watery shimmers and atmospheric effects.

LADY WITH A PARASOL, right, 1886

Monet painted two versions of this motif, showing Suzanne Hoschedé standing on a hillock at the Ile aux Orties, near Giverny. In the first version the girl is facing to the artist's right, in the second she faces to the left. Monet's purpose here was not really portraiture but a study of light and how it was affected by the different poses adopted by the model. One is irresistibly reminded of the portrait of Camille in a similar attitude, painted during the Argenteuil period.

Suzanne, strikingly pretty, later married the American painter Theodore Butler. She died in 1899 at the age of thirty-one, and her loss threw Alice and the rest of the family into despair. She had been the liveliest of all the daughters and a great favourite. Her husband later married her older sister Marthe.

Monet refused to be parted from the two pictures of Suzanne. They were still in his studio when he died, and were presented to the Louvre in 1927 by Michel Monet.

Claude Monet had no daughters of his own but several stepdaughters, the children of his second wife.   The girl painting is Blanche, and her sister Suzanne is sitting on the grass reading.

Blanche, who later married Monet's elder son Jean, often used to accompany her stepfather on his expeditions, helping to carry his materials.   Watching him at work she was inspired to try her own hand at painting in the summer of 1882, while they were on holiday at Pourville near Dieppe.   She was a sensitive and intelligent girl and proved to have talent.   A few of her best canvases are in the finest traditions of Impressionism.   She abandoned painting when her husband died in 1914, but took it up again twelve years later, after the death of Claude Monet, and continued to paint right up to her death in 1947.   The long interval is explained by the fact that for more than a decade she looked after her stepfather, relieving him of all practical concerns.   Georges Clemenceau called her the Blue Angel.

Suzanne, the youngest of the Hoschedé daughters, was Monet's favourite model.   He was very fond of these lively, affectionate girls, and would often relax by playing them at croquet or reading aloud to them.

'There on the narrow and swiftly-running River Epte, among the reeds, in the pale shadow of arching greenery, he (Claude Monet) brings alive human figures too. A light boat bears two *(sic)* girls dressed in pink, one in the bows, one at the oars. This is a harmony of sombre green and vivid pink, a portrait of young girls in the flower of their youth, delicious and fleeting apparitions.' This evocative description was provided by Gustave Geffroy in his biography of Monet.

The effect the painter was trying to achieve was not only the contrast of the pale silhouettes against the dark vegetation, but the eddies of iridescence created in the transparent water by pieces of weed bobbing in the current. It was a theme that obsessed Monet. Three years after painting this canvas, he wrote to Geffroy: 'I have had another shot at something that's quite impossible, water with weed waving below the surface.' Monet was often to be seen on the banks of the River Epte or by his lily pond, studying the effects of transparency. Sometimes he would stand there like a statue for minutes on end.

The three girls with fishing rods are Blanche, Suzanne and Germaine Hoschedé. It was quite out of the question for Monet to employ professional models. Once he had declared his intention to do so and was informed by his jealous wife: 'The moment a model sets foot in this house, I leave.'

This idyllic scene is one of Monet's most appealing works. He loved to represent the youthful innocence and high spirits of his stepdaughters and painted several variations on a boating theme—the visual counterpart to Debussy's 'En Bateau', composed at about this time.

The canvas was bought by the Princesse de Polignac, a close friend of Marcel Proust. It is likely that he learned through her to appreciate Monet's painting, to which there are several allusions in his books.

HAYSTACKS, AT THE END OF SUMMER, 1890

With the *Haystacks* series, started in the late summer of 1890 and completed the following spring, Monet entered on a new period in his work. For the next thirty years he was to concentrate almost exclusively on a few subjects: Haystacks, Poplars, Rouen Cathedral, the Houses of Parliament, the Waterlilies. What interested him henceforth was the expression of transient appearances—the motif itself would be unvarying and viewed always from the same angle, only the light would change, depending on the season, the weather and the time of day.

His method was to work on several canvases at once, devoting perhaps no more than a few minutes at a time to any one of them. It was necessary to work swiftly to capture the 'moment' before it dissolved. In this he was greatly assisted by his stepdaughter Blanche, who would slide the canvases into position on his easel.

On 7 October, in full flight, he wrote to Gustave Geffroy: '...the further I get, the more I see how much work it will need to convey what I am searching for: "instantaneity", and above all the external "envelope", the same light spread everywhere...'

The series of 25 canvases was completed by the end of the winter of 1891. Some 15 of these were exhibited by Durand-Ruel in May. For the first time there was no hostile reaction, only unanimous praise. Gustave Geffroy's preface to the exhibition catalogue is a string of hyperboles, but it also contains a sensitive account of these 'haystacks in an empty field'.

The *Haystacks* series had a marked influence on the younger painters, particularly the Fauves, Derain and Vlaminck. For Kandinsky, seeing examples in Moscow, and later in Munich, was one of the decisive experiences of his life. He wrote in his memoirs: 'What suddenly became clear to me was the unsuspected power of the palette, which I had not understood before and which surpassed my wildest dreams.'

The success of the series solved Monet's problems at a stroke: most of the canvases were sold for as much as 1,000 francs, and Monet's prices in general began to rise steeply. This financial coup enabled him to buy outright the house and grounds at Giverny and to start constructing a waterlily pond.

ROUEN CATHEDRAL, 1892

This canvas shows the main façade of Rouen Cathedral and the Tour d'Albane in full sunlight. Monet had never before laboured so greatly, or become so depressed, as he did on these two expeditions to Rouen, in 1892-93, to paint the cathedral. His letters are full of references to his low spirits and fatigue. 'I am broken, I can do no more... I have had a night filled with nightmares: the cathedral was falling down on top of me...', he wrote to Alice Hoschedé on 3 April 1892. And again to Durand-Ruel, ten days later: 'I am utterly dejected and dissatisfied with what I have done, I have aimed too high and only succeeded in spoiling what was good.' There is the same tone of impotence and despair in the letters he wrote in 1893 at the time of his second visit. Again he felt he was being too ambitious. As in his previous series, the *Haystacks* and the *Poplars*, he was trying to capture the evanescence of appearances, but the old grey stone seemed to be changing before his eyes. So he would work over what he had done, building up the impasto, giving the canvas an almost abstract character and a grainy texture.

Over the thirty paintings the presentation of the façade varies, sometimes viewed frontally, sometimes at a slight angle. This depended on Monet's vantage point, which was either above a lingerie shop or on the first floor of a dress shop. One can only imagine what the customers must have felt as they came for a fitting and saw this bearded gentleman, pipe in mouth, painting away by an open window in the depths of winter. Monet was oblivious to all the distractions, all his energies were bent on observing the play of light on the ancient stone. The work exhausted him, and in April 1893 he simply called a halt, returned to Giverny and went to bed for three days.

It was not until May 1895, after the pictures had been finished in the studio, that the 'cathedrals' were exhibited by Durand-Ruel. Pissarro, Degas, Renoir and Cézanne were all dumbfounded, as too was the art critic Georges Clemenceau, who wrote in *La Justice*: 'Monet's eye is our precursor, it sees beyond us and guides us in a visual education which renders our perception of the universe more penetrating and sensitive... The true wonder of Monet is that he sees how the very stones vibrate, and shows them to us, vibrant.'

This picture belongs to one of the less well-known of Monet's series—the reason being that the majority of the seventeen canvases are dispersed in museums outside France.

The 'morning' shows the river waters shimmering in the first rays of light of an August day. While painting the series, Monet was obliged to rise well before dawn. Blanche or one of the other Hoschedé children would go with him to carry his canvases. Together they would make for the confluence of the Seine and the Epte, where there was an old boat-shed that Monet used for doing repairs. From the lack of foreground, and the angle of the perspective along the river and its banks, it seems likely that these canvases were painted from the studio-boat he had owned since his days in Argenteuil.

Monet's method was the same as for his other series: he would work, a little at a time, on several canvases at once.

Although Durand-Ruel bought several of the 'mornings', Monet chose to have them exhibited by Georges Petit, the chief competitor of the dealer to whom he owed so much. In business matters Monet was not a sentimentalist.

WATERLILIES, GREEN HARMONY, 1899

A few months after becoming the owner of the property where he had already lived for ten years, Monet purchased a piece of marshland across the road and declared his intention to construct a water garden. There were numerous problems, since the villagers of Giverny complained to the authorities that the pond, linked to the Epte, would poison the river. But, permission once granted, the work went ahead quickly, and Monet was soon able to start creating the water garden that was to occupy most of his thoughts and energies for the next three decades.

Early in 1895, before he left for Norway, he painted his first view of the Japanese bridge that spanned the pond, but it was not until 1898 that he started work in earnest. Most of the canvases he painted at this time are square and show the Japanese bridge and the water surface dotted with lilies—Nymphea is the botanical name for the common white waterlily.

In those early works the sky does not appear except as a reflection: the perspective is provided by the plants edging the pond and the weeping willows.

Ten canvases of this first series were exhibited at Durand-Ruel's gallery. The occasion was euphoric. Even Degas, normally less than enthusiastic about Monet's work (he said he wished the police would pepper the *plein-air* painters with shot), was ecstatic, and wanted to buy one of the pictures. Whether he did or not is unclear, since the painting is not included in the auction catalogue listing the works in his studio in 1918. It is even possible that he destroyed it: it would not have been the first time.

Waterlilies, Green Harmony was bought by Isaac de Camondo the day after Durand-Ruel's exhibition opened. Eight years later he bequeathed his magnificent collection—which included fourteen Monets—to the Louvre.

This sumptuous canvas is a very recent addition to the Jeu de Paume collection. It shows one of the narrow paths leading up the garden to the house, the pink roughcast walls and grey-blue shutters of which can be seen in the background.

Here Monet's prized irises are in full flower—but in this garden there were flowers of one sort or another all the year round. It was maintained by six under-gardeners working under the direction of a head-gardener appointed on the recommendation of the Comtesse Greffuhle. Taking the seasons carefully into account, Monet designed it to provide the coloured masses he wanted for his paintings. His aim was to achieve an effect of great simplicity, with the paths crossing at right-angles; in this the garden was untypical of its day. Monet detested double blooms or exotic plants and, on the advice of Truffaut and Vilmorin, chose from the common flowers, principally those with long stems such as peonies, poppies, sunflowers and asters. Only the red and orange nasturtiums ran riot alongside the paths. The effect was striking, and in his memoirs René Gimpel recalls the impression it made on him when he first visited Giverny. 'You would need to be a Maeterlinck to describe a garden that resembles no other, first because it is composed of the commonest of flowers, and then because they grow to such an inordinate height. I don't believe there is a single one that flowers at less than a metre high... It is not a meadow but a virgin forest of flowers, all in bold colours; no delicate pinks or pale blue, just reds and blues.'

We know that this garden was described to Marcel Proust by his friends, but unfortunately he never saw it.

After the death of Blanche Hoschedé-Monet in 1947, the garden was left untended, but in 1980 it was recreated, with the help of a generous gift from an American admirer of Monet's work. He became interested in the project in the course of conversations with Gerald van der Kemp, the custodian of the property.

It is now possible to visit the house, also restored, and to walk through the garden, experiencing the atmosphere of the place where Claude Monet lived and worked for more than forty years.

YELLOW IRISES WITH PINK CLOUD, 1903

As though as a distraction from his major obsession, Monet would sometimes break off from his waterlily canvases and paint wonderfully vivid studies of the water irises that grew at the edges of the pond. He had a particular love of irises and always regretted their short flowering season. In the days before his death he was expecting some Japanese irises that a friend had promised to send him from Tokyo. It was all he could think of.

Painted quickly, this canvas demonstrates one curious feature typical of Monet's works: the edges are not finished. This is true of most of the paintings done from the motif; Monet would normally finish them in the studio, usually when he added his signature. The incomplete character of a canvas pleased him, he saw it as a mark of spontaneity.

Claude Monet retained a great affection for London since his first visit in 1870-71, during the Franco-Prussian War. He loved the murky light and the famous fog, an atmospheric blend of mist and smoke from the coal fires with which the Londoners of the time heated their homes. He returned there on several occasions, but notably in 1899, 1900 and 1901, when he visited his son Michel, in England to learn the language. The other purpose of his visits was of course to paint. Monet did not speak English and yet felt at home in London, the more so as he had a long-standing friendship with Whistler and Sargent. Installed at the Savoy, he could look out from his balcony over the Thames to the Waterloo and Charing Cross Bridges, and in the distance the Houses of Parliament.

Although he started most of his hundred or so London pictures *in situ*, working from the motif, we know that the majority were finished in the studio—and indeed it seems from Monet's letters that some were done entirely from memory at Giverny. In March 1903 he wrote to Durand-Ruel: 'No, I am not in London, except in spirit, but working hard on my canvases, which are giving me a lot of trouble.'

This view of the Houses of Parliament, in tones of bluey-green, has a violence of brushwork and heightened colouring that could legitimately be called Fauve. At the time, neither Matisse, Derain nor Vlaminck could have equalled it. The original line is completely submerged and the silhouette of the building is expressed in long whiplash strokes of colour. Only the waters of the Thames are painted in broad horizontal dabs—like the sea in *Impression: Sunrise.* Probably in this sequence Monet comes closest to achieving the 'instantaneity' he had sought since the *Haystacks.*

Others of the London canvases look back to an earlier style. In attempting to convey the precise quality of the fog and mist, Monet at times resembles Turner, although without the romantic effects favoured by the English artist.

WATERLILIES, 1907

A round canvas such as this is a rarity in Monet's *œuvre*; there is also a companion-piece in the Musée de Vernon, which the painter presented to the town in May 1925, an unusual gesture of generosity on his part.

The Saint-Étienne 'tondo' was bought direct from the artist in 1924, for the sum of 30,000 francs.

Both these works, which are very similar, demonstrate an extremely fluid technique coupled with transparency of colour. Because of his love of the effects of transparency Monet was always fanatically insistent that the water in the pond should be absolutely pure, so that the reflections of the sky and clouds formed an undistorted image. One of the gardeners was charged with keeping the pond always in perfect condition.

WATERLILIES, 1908

This utterly perfect painting is one of the 236 recorded canvases in the *Waterlilies* sequence. It belongs to the group painted in 1907-08, 48 of which were exhibited at Durand-Ruel's gallery in May/June 1909 under the title chosen by Monet, 'Les Nymphéas, paysage d'eau'.

Overwhelmed with enthusiasm, Romain Rolland wrote to Monet: 'When I feel sickened by the mediocrity of present-day literature and music, I have only to turn my eyes to painting, where works like your *Waterlilies* blossom, in order to reconcile myself to our artistic epoch and to feel it is the equal of any other that has gone before.'

Probably it was the success of this exhibition, and the regret voiced on all sides that such an ensemble should be broken up and dispersed, that gave Monet the idea of using waterlilies as a basis for a huge decorative work, one that would literally enclose the spectator on all sides. In June of that year he explained the outline of the project to Roger-Marx. It was not, however, until the time of the First World War, on the insistence of Georges Clemenceau, that he actually implemented his plans.

In 1916 a specially designed studio was built, large enough to accomodate the vast surfaces. The preliminary stage of painting was accomplished with remarkable speed. But then began the process of reworking and retouching the 19 panels, a task that was to occupy Monet for the remaining years of his life—and that in spite of the double cataract that affected his eyesight until it was operated on in 1923.

When Monet died on 6 December 1926, his artistic legacy was complete.

THE GRAND CANAL, VENICE, 1908

This classic view of Venice was painted from the vantage point of the Accademia bridge, and shows the Salute in the middle ground and behind it the tower of the Doges' Palace. Like Manet, who painted the same scene in 1875, Claude Monet used the mooring-poles to counterbalance the horizontal strokes defining the canal itself. Although the Salute is prominent, one senses that it was the painting of the water that truly interested him. It has been pointed out that the pole intersecting the canvas two thirds across its width is in compliance with the golden section. One wonders if Monet, who prided himself on being a painter of instinct ('painting as the bird sings'), was aware of such refinements?

The lengthy trip to Venice in the autumn of 1908 was unique in one respect: Monet was accompanied by his wife Alice. Previously he had always gone alone on his painting expeditions, whether to Belle-Ile, or Étretat, Bordighera or Antibes.

On this particular visit he worked hard—there was an exhibition held by Durand-Ruel in 1912 of 29 paintings from Venice—but one deduces from his letters that he also enjoyed himself as a tourist. 'I am spending some delightful days here,' he wrote to Gustave Geffroy, 'almost forgetting I am not the old man I am in reality.'

Installed in the Grand Hotel Britannia on the Riva degli Schavoni, he could see from his balcony the comings and goings on the Lagoon and the steamers leaving for the Lido and Chioggia. He visited the museums and churches and strolled in St Mark's Square. There is a photo of him with Alice feeding the pigeons.

The canvases started in Venice and completed in the studio on his return, together with some executed entirely at Giverny, reveal that Venice did not make him change the habits of a lifetime: he viewed the monuments and façades of the palaces in just the same way as he had studied the front of Rouen Cathedral, noting the effects of the light playing over it, interested only in the way the architecture was transmuted by the alterations in the atmosphere. Decidedly, with Canaletto or Guardi he had nothing in common, although there are distinct analogies with Turner. In these Venice paintings Monet's vision tends more to Romanticism than usual, recalling not only Turner but Whistler, who loved Venice and had talked to Monet about it with such enthusiasm that he decided he had to see it for himself. 'What a tragedy not to have come here when I was younger,' he wrote in a letter to Geffroy.

When he left he declared he would return the following year, but Alice's illness and death relegated that ambition to the back of his mind.

LIST OF PLATES

(80×50 cm). Musée d'Orsay, Paris.

99 : Parisians in the Parc Monceau, 1878 (73×55 cm).
Metropolitan Museum of Art, New York.

101 : The Ice-Floes, 1880 (60×100 cm).
Musée d'Orsay, Paris.

103 : Ile Saint-Martin, Vétheuil, 1880 (73×60 cm).
Metropolitan Museum of Art, New York.

105 : Girl seated beneath a Willow, 1880 (81×60 cm).
National Gallery of Art, Washington.

107 : Monet's Garden at Vétheuil, 1881 (150×120 cm).
National Gallery of Art, Washington.

109 : The Douanier's Cottage, 1882 (60×73 cm).
Musée Boymans-Van Beuningen, Rotterdam.

111 : The Beach and Cliffs at Étretat, 1883 (66×81 cm).
Musée d'Orsay, Paris.

113 : Storm on Belle-Ile, 1886 (65×81 cm).
Musée d'Orsay, Paris.

115 : Lady with a Parasol, right, 1886 (131×88 cm).
Musée d'Orsay, Paris.

117 : Blanche Monet painting, 1887 (130×97 cm).
County Museum of Art, Los Angeles.

119 : The Boat at Giverny, 1887 (98×131 cm).
Musée d'Orsay, Paris.

121 : Haystacks, at the End of Summer, 1890 (60×100 cm).
Musée d'Orsay, Paris.

123 : Rouen Cathedral, 1892 (106×73 cm).
Musée d'Orsay, Paris.

125 : Morning on the Seine, 1897.
Metropolitan Museum of Art, New York.

127 : Waterlilies, Green Harmony, 1899 (89×93 cm).
Musée d'Orsay, Paris.

129 : The Garden at Giverny, 1900 (81×92 cm).
Musée d'Orsay, Paris.

131 : Yellow Irises with Pink Cloud, 1903.
Collection particulière, New York.

133 : The Houses of Parliament, 1904 (81×92 cm).

Musée Marmottan, Paris.

135 : Waterlilies, 1907 (∅ 80 cm).
Musée d'Art et d'Industrie, Saint-Étienne.

137 : Waterlilies, 1908 (92×89 cm).
Collection particulière, Zurich.

139 : The Grand Canal, Venice, 1908.
Museum of Fine Art, Boston.

SHORT BIBLIOGRAPHY

BLUNDEN, Maria and Godfrey: *Journal de l'impressionnisme*, Skira, Geneva, 1970.
COTTE, Sabine: *Monet*, Henri Scrépel, Paris, 1974.
CRESPELLE, Jean-Paul: *Les Maîtres de la Belle Époque*, Hachette, Paris, 1966.
DURET, Théodore: *Les Peintres impressionnistes*, Paris, 1878.
FELS, Marthe DE: *La Vie de Claude Monet*, Paris, 1929.
GAUGUIN, Paul: *Racontars de Rapin*, Falaize, Paris, 1951.
GEFFROY, Gustave: *Monet, sa vie, son œuvre*, Macula, Paris, 1980.
GIMPEL, René: *Journal d'un collectionneur*, Calman-Lévy, Paris, 1963.
GORDON, Robert and FORGE, Andrew: *Monet*, Flammarion, Paris, 1984.
HOSCHEDÉ, Jean-Pierre: *Claude Monet, ce mal connu*, Cailler, Geneva, 1960 (2 vol.).
MIRBEAU, Octave: *Des Artistes*, Flammarion, Paris, 1922.
Hommage à Claude Monet, Catalogue of the exhibition at the Grand Palais, Paris, 1980.
MONNERET, Sophie: *L'Impressionnisme et son époque*, Daniel Filipacchi, Paris, 1978.
NATANSON, Thadée: *Peints à leur tour*, Albin Michel, Paris, 1948.
RAGON, Michel: *Les Grands Peintres racontés par eux-mêmes*, Albin Michel, Paris, 1965.
REWALD, John: *Histoire de l'impressionnisme*, Albin Michel, Paris, 1955.
ROGER-MARX, Claude: *Monet*, Fernand Hazan, Paris, 1959.
DEGAND, L. and ROUART, D.: *Claude Monet*, Skira, Geneva, 1958.
ROUART, Denis and REY, Jean-Dominique: *Monet, Nymphéas*, Fernand Hazan, Paris, 1972.
TAILLANDIER, Yvon: *Claude Monet*, Flammarion, Paris, n.d.
VOLLARD, Ambroise: *Souvenirs d'un marchand de tableaux*, Albin Michel, Paris, 1937.
WILDENSTEIN, Daniel: *Monet*, Diffusion Princesse, Paris, 1974.
WILDENSTEIN, Daniel: *Claude Monet, biographie et catalogue raisonné*, 3 vol., Bibliothèque des Arts, Lausanne-Paris, 1974.
ZOLA, Émile: *L'Œuvre*, Garnier-Flammarion, Paris, 1974.

PHOTOGRAPH CREDITS

CHRONOLOGY

1840
Birth of Oscar-Claude Monet, in rue Laffitte, Paris.

1845
The Monet family moves to Le Havre, where Claude's father works in the wholesale grocery business run by his brother-in-law.

1846
Monet draws caricatures of local celebrities in Le Havre.

1858
Paints on the Normandy coast with Eugène Boudin.

1859
Visits Paris, consults Troyon about his future.

1861-62
Military service in Algeria in the *Chasseurs d'Afrique*. Contracts typhoid and is sent to convalesce in France. His aunt purchases a replacement.

1862
Meets Jongkind at Sainte-Adresse, accompanies him on painting expeditions.

1862-63
Goes to Paris, attends Gleyre's studio and meets Renoir, Bazille and Sisley.

1864
At Easter, goes to Chailly-en-Bière with Renoir and Bazille. Stays in Honfleur, with Bazille.

1865
Two landscapes accepted for the Salon. Starts *Le Déjeuner sur l'herbe*. Meets Courbet. Autumn in Trouville.

1866
The portrait of Camille, *Woman in a Green Dress*, is a huge success at the Salon. Favourable article by Zola. Becomes a friend of Manet. Lives in Sèvres with Camille. Starts work on *Women in the Garden*.

1867
Women in the Garden rejected by the Salon, and bought by Bazille. Money problems. Birth of Jean Monet, in Paris. Paints *The Terrace at Sainte-Adresse*.

1868
Painting accepted for the Salon. Income from commissions given by Monsieur Gaudibert, a collector in Le Havre. Holiday in Gloton, with Camille.

1869
Rejection by the Salon. Lives in Saint-Michel, near Bougival, and paints scenes at the 'Grenouillère', with Renoir. Severe financial difficulties.

1870
Marries Camille Doncieux, on 26 June. In late September, flees to London, leaving Camille and son in Trouville. In London, introduced by Daubigny to the dealer Durand-Ruel, whose purchases ensure him an adequate income. Discovers Constable and Turner.

1871
In June, goes to Zaandam in Holland. Returns to Paris, moves to Argenteuil in November.

1872-73
Paints the Seine at Argenteuil. Trips to Rouen and Le Havre. Meetings of the Impressionists-to-be at the Café Guerbois.

1874
On 13 April, opening of an exhibition of work by the independent painters, in rooms lent by the photographer Nadar. Monet's *Impression: Sunrise* gives the movement its name. Further financial difficulties. Trip to Holland.

1876
Summer in the château de Rottenbourg, at Montgeron, owned by the collector Ernest Hoschedé. Monet paints four decorative panels for the salon. Starts the series *Gare Saint-Lazare.*

1877
Zola writes in praise of the station paintings shown at the third Impressionist exhibition. Surrounded by debts, the family is forced to leave Argenteuil.

1878
Birth of Michel Monet, in Paris. Move to Vétheuil, with the Hoschedé household.

1879
Death of Camille, aged thirty-two, on 5 September.

1880
During the terrible winter, Monet paints the break-up of the ice on the Seine, inaugurating a new phase of his career. His *Lavacourt* landscape is accepted for the Salon. First one-man-show, at the La Vie Moderne gallery.

1881
Early in the year, Durand-Ruel resumes his purchases. Numerous trips to Dieppe, Fécamp, Pourville, Varangeville, Étretat. Move to Poissy. Alice Hoschedé runs the joint household.

1882
Lengthy visit to Pourville. Takes part in seventh Impressionist exhibition.

1883
Visits to Le Havre and Étretat. Move to Giverny, in April. Late December, travelling on the Riviera, with Renoir.

1884
January to April, in Bordighera. In August, visit to Étretat.

1885
Exhibition at gallery run by Georges Petit, Durand-Ruel's rival. Becomes a friend of Maupassant, whom he meets at Étretat.

1886-87
Étretat. Durand-Ruel exhibits works by the Impressionists in his New York gallery. Short trip to Holland. Lengthy visit to Belle-Ile. Meeting with Geffroy. Visit to London.

1888
January to May, in Antibes and Juan-les-Pins. Ten Antibes canvases exhibited, in June, by Théo van Gogh. Trip to London.

1889
Visits the Creuse, staying for three months in Fresselines with the poet Maurice Rollinat. Monet-Rodin exhibition in June, organized by Georges Petit. Campaign to purchase Manet's *Olympia* for the Louvre.

1890
Buys the house at Giverny.

1891-92
Haystacks and *Poplars* series.

1892
In Rouen, starts the *Rouen Cathedral* series. In July, marries Alice Hoschedé.

1893
Continues the series of *Rouen Cathedral.*

1894
Work starts on digging out the lilypond. Cézanne stays in Giverny.

1895
Trip to Norway.

1896-97
Expeditions on the Normandy coast.

1899
Trip to London.

1900
Further trip to London. Durand-Ruel exhibits ten *Waterlilies* canvases.

1901
February to April, in London.

1904
The London paintings exhibited by Durand-Ruel.

1908
Monet and Alice visit Venice.

1909
Major exhibition of *Waterlilies* at Durand-Ruel's gallery.

1911
Death of Alice Monet, on 19 May.

1912
Exhibition by Durand-Ruel of the Venice pictures.

1914
Death of Jean Monet, on 10 February.

1916
Construction of a vast studio to house the large *Waterlilies* panels.

1922
On 12 April, Monet signs the deed of gift by which the 19 *Waterlilies* panels will pass to the state.

1923
Monet undergoes an operation to remove a double cataract.

1926
Death of Claude Monet, on 5 December.

1927
Opening of the *Waterlilies* rooms at the Orangerie in the Tuileries Gardens.

1966
Michel Monet leaves to the Académie des Beaux-Arts 137 paintings by his father and the other Impressionists, subsequently placed on permanent display, with *Impression: Sunrise*, at the Musée Marmottan.